GHOSTLY
TYNE & WEAR

ROB KIRKUP

The History Press

To my wife, Jo.

First published 2009
Reprinted 2013

The History Press
The Mill, Brimscombe Port
Stroud, Gloucestershire, GL5 2QG
www.thehistorypress.co.uk

© Rob Kirkup, 2009

The right of Rob Kirkup to be identified as the Author
of this work has been asserted in accordance with the
Copyrights, Designs and Patents Act 1988.

British Library Cataloguing in Publication Data.
A catalogue record for this book is available from the British Library.

ISBN 978 0 7509 5109 8

Typesetting and origination by The History Press
Printed in Great Britain

Contents

Foreword

Ghost stories are an extremely important part of our heritage. They often reflect famous and well documented historical events. More usually, however, the occurrences that ghost stories recall are not so well known, and precious little historical documentation survives about them. Indeed, there is little doubt that the events that have given rise to many ghostly tales would have been long forgotten were it not for the fact that the protagonist who was involved in a bygone saga has for some reason found themselves condemned to haunt the location at which they either died or suffered some trauma. Thus ghost stories are often, in my opinion, not just accounts of an actual haunting, but they can also provide an insightful record of historical characters and events. As such they are an important and valuable resource.

I also think that ghost stories are the last bastion of the oral tradition. In my researches around Britain and Ireland I have, on many occasions, found myself in an old inn or hotel bar late at night when somebody has brought up the subject of ghosts. There is often a mixed reaction with some people admitting to be fervent believers in the supernatural and others claiming to be ardent sceptics. Yet within a few moments of the subject of ghosts being brought up everyone in the room begins recounting their own experiences of the supernatural and the great British tradition of storytelling has everyone chatting, laughing and trying to spook each other!

Of course these story-telling sessions are impulse sessions which are, more often than not, soon forgotten as everyone goes their separate ways. For a ghost story to find its way into the wider arena of local tradition it needs to be collected and written down. The problem is that there are very few people willing to do this and even fewer who take the trouble to go to a location, interview the people who have seen the ghost and then take the trouble to accurately investigate the history to try and find a possible explanation for the haunting or even, on occasion, identify exactly who the ghost is, or was.

A lack of well researched, well informed and well told ghost stories is something that will not occur in *Ghostly Tyne & Wear*. Rob has put together an excellent A–Z of the ghostly happenings in the area and the finished publication is a great, and in parts chilling, read. He has done a superb job at researching each of the haunted locations and has taken the trouble to bring his accounts right up to date by interviewing the people who now live or work at each of the locations featured.

One of the stories that I found particularly gripping was that of the ghost of the great comedy actor Sid James who is reputed to haunt the Sunderland Empire Theatre. I can actually remember hearing the news report that Sid James had died on stage. However, I had no idea where the theatre was at which the tragedy occurred. Rob recounts the events of the night on which Sid James died and then provides details of the haunting. It is a perfect example of how his book seamlessly welds together both historical and contemporary accounts in such away that you find yourself just wanting to turn the page to find out what happened next.

However, Rob doesn't stop there; he also provides the intrepid ghost hunter with every detail they will need to pay a visit to and/or learn more about a property, by providing full addresses, telephone numbers, directions, opening hours and even the websites of his featured properties. Such attention to detail really does place Rob's book above the standard of the average local ghost study and it is destined to become a classic, valuable, and no doubt well thumbed, inclusion in the library of anyone who enjoys ghost stories.

Richard Jones, 2009

Acknowledgements

I would like to begin by thanking my family for their support throughout the writing of *Ghostly Tyne & Wear*; in particular my wife Jo, my parents Tom and Emily, and my brother Thomas. I would also like to express my gratitude to my in-laws, Michael and Patricia, my brother-in-law James, and Norman and Margaret, Jo's grandparents.

Many thanks go to John Crozier and Andrew Markwell for accompanying me on the countless trips out to theatres, pubs, castles, pubs, museums, and pubs, researching each location, and taking the photographs that you see throughout this book.

My close friends have offered no end of encouragement during this project and I would like to thank them all; in particular Dan Armstrong, Harry Dalton, Ryan Elwell, Brian Moore, Peter Slater, John Gray, Andrew Davidson, Paul Morton, Richard Stokoe, Paul Bicker, Karl Railton, David Henderson, and Mark and Lesley Harrison.

I have spent many, many hours reading books on the subject of the paranormal written by Richard Jones, and I was thrilled when he agreed to write the foreword for *Ghostly Tyne & Wear*. Thanks Richard.

I am indebted to the staff and owners of the locations included in this book; they could not possibly have been more helpful. I am grateful to them all for allowing their properties to be included.

A number of people were kind enough to talk to me about their personal experiences at the locations that I chose to include in this book. I would like to extend my gratitude to them all; Suzanne Hitchinson, Darren Ritson, Carole Chipchase, Pauline Haughey, Paul Stothard, Jay Brown, Pat Adamswright, Mike Hallowell, Tommy Harrison, Steven Hickman, Liz Harrison, Steve Taylor, Ethel Turnbull, Lee Foster, Melvyn James, and Paul and Pam Cajiao.

Last, but by no means least, I would like to thank everyone at The History Press, Matilda Richards in particular, for the faith they have showed in me, and their support and guidance throughout.

The Tyne Bridge. (Photograph by Ian McWilliams)

Introduction

As I write this it is nearing midnight on Hallowe'en, the night on which many believe the dead return and walk amongst the living. Outside the streets are eerily quiet; the heavy rain is rapping at my window and the wind is howling through the trees. However, the only run-in I've had this evening with brain-eating zombies, cackling witches, and blood-sucking vampires has come in the form of the never-ending stream of horror films on television, and the constant knocking at my door by children in fancy dress asking for sweets or loose change. It's fascinating to think that, despite our modern traditions of bobbing for apples and ghoulish outfits, the origins of Hallowe'en date back to the ancient Celtic festival of Samhain. The Celts believed, as we do now, that the ghosts of the departed returned to Earth, they also thought that on the night of Samhain the veil between this world and the next was at its thinnest. To appease these spirits they would light a huge bonfire and burn bones from freshly slaughtered animals while wearing costumes made of animal skin. They would then light their hearth fires from the sacred bonfire, believing this would prevent evil spirits from entering their homes. The Celts believed in ghosts unquestionably, but over 2,000 years later in the year 2008, it's a question which divides mankind like no other. Do *you* believe in ghosts?

I was thrilled to be asked to write a book as a follow-up to *Ghostly Northumberland*, and, in my opinion, Tyne and Wear was the perfect area to write about. I live in the region and there are literally hundreds of haunted places with widely varied histories; from locations with horrific, bloody pasts, dating back many hundreds of years, to relatively new buildings with little history to speak of, but still home to all manner of supernatural phenomena. The Centre of Life in Newcastle-upon-Tyne is a perfect example; opening in April 2006, not many would consider the popular science centre as a building that fits the description of the traditional 'haunted house'. However, what few people know is that the centre was built on the site of Newcastle's first hospital, and when the foundations of the centre were being dug, hundreds of human bones were discovered and removed. The builders started hearing unusual 'other-worldly' noises, and tools and equipment began to go missing. Only when the bones were reinterred in consecrated ground did the disturbances cease.

Tyne and Wear has such a wealth of places worthy of inclusion, that one of the hardest aspects of compiling this book was narrowing the locations down to the places that feature in these pages. Every one of them is open to the public, and each chapter includes a visitor information section to help you plan your trip should you dare to visit them for yourself.

Bear in mind that throughout the ages, virtually every square inch of Tyne and Wear is likely to have witnessed violent murder, executions, plague, or brutal invasions by the Vikings, the Romans, and the Scots; so there are many, many more places that are liable to be home to all manner of paranormal happenings. If you live in Tyne and Wear maybe your local pub is haunted, or church nearby, or even your place of work. Perhaps you're not even safe from the spirits of those long dead in the one place you would expect to find sanctuary – your home . . .

The photographs throughout this book are the authors own, unless otherwise stated.

Rob Kirkup, 2009

A-Z of Haunted Locations in Tyne &c. Wear

Angel View Inn

*O*verlooking the world-famous Angel of the North is the Angel View Inn. It was originally built as a farmhouse and stables, and the original stonework of the buildings can still be seen. Today it is a twenty-seven bedroom hotel, restaurant, conference and banqueting venue.

There is a legend at the inn of a young girl who was tending to a horse in the stables when the horse bolted and kicked out, hitting her in the face and killing her instantly. Is it said that she walks the corridors of the Angel View Inn, and those who have seen her have described her as having a gaping hole where her face should be. Staff members have also witnessed a man wandering the building on a number of occasions, most commonly near room 14; upon being approached he vanishes.

One of the current housekeepers was cleaning one of the rooms; she cleaned the bathroom, and then made the bed. She heard a noise in the bathroom and when she went back in all of the taps had been turned on fully. The same housekeeper had finished cleaning room 15, and as she left the room and was closing the door, she noticed an imprint on the bed in the shape of a person lying down, with an impression in the pillow where a head appeared to be.

One night, a couple staying in room 16 complained that they had been kept awake for hours by the sound of children running and laughing outside their room. There were no children staying in the hotel that night.

I spent an evening in the company of Tommy Harrison, who has worked as the night porter at the Angel View Inn for the previous six years, and has experienced some of the ghostly goings-on for himself during the many nights he has spent there. This is what he told me:

The previous night porter had no knowledge of the legend of the 'faceless' girl, and one night he sat down and started drawing as he often did. He drew a young girl with a dark void where her face should have been.

There was one night when a woman and her two young children were staying in room 9. She awoke during the night and one of her sons was sat at the bottom of her bed. She then realized to her horror that both of her children were fast asleep and that the child sat at the bottom of her bed was in fact a ghost. She was very shaken and upset.

The Angel View Inn. (By kind permission of the Angel View Inn)

There have been a lot of disturbances in the kitchen with pots and pans being thrown about when the room has been empty. We had a medium stay at the Angel View Inn and we were told that the building is home to six spirits.

It is interesting that the Angel of the North itself is believed to be haunted by the ghost of a Second World War Nazi recruitment officer, despite the 66ft-high landmark having only been erected in 1998. A number of visitors to the Antony Gormley sculpture have reported seeing the phantom, most commonly in the twilight, just after the last traces of sunlight have faded beyond the horizon.

Room 9; the room in which a lady customer woke during the night to find the ghost of a young boy sat at the bottom of her bed. (By kind permission of the Angel View Inn)

Antony Gormley's Angel of the North.

Visitor Information

Address:
The Angel View Inn
Low Eighton
Gateshead
Tyne and Wear
NE9 7UB

Tel: 0191 4103219
Website: www.angelviewinn.co.uk
Email: reception@angelviewinn.co.uk

Opening Hours: Food is served in the restaurant Monday–Saturday midday– 9 p.m. Sunday lunch is served midday–6 p.m. Main menu served from 6 p.m.

How to Get There: From A1 north or south follow the brown tourist signs for the Angel of the North. At the immediate roundabout take the exit signposted Wrekenton onto the B1295. Take the first left into the Angel View Inn car park

Additional Information:
- For further information about the Angel View Inn's facilities for banqueting and functions, please visit their website or call on the number above
- The Angel View Inn also caters for wedding receptions; further information is available on their website
- The hotel offers standard doubles and twins, and also superior doubles. All rooms are en-suite and many have stunning views of the Angel of the North. Family rooms are also available. Breakfast is included

Arbeia Roman Fort

A rbeia is the remains of a large Roman fort in South Shields built in around AD 158 on a low headland overlooking the River Tyne. Human occupation on this land predates the arrival of the Roman in Britain by many centuries. Archaeological evidence of the the earliest settlements date back to 3000–4000 BC. An Iron-Age roundhouse dating from 400 BC was recently excavated in the south-east corner of the site.

The Roman army had a firm grasp on the north east of England by the time the Roman fort was built in the second century. The fort covered a site of 4.1 acres and was home to 120 cavalry and 480 foot soldiers. By the early third century, the garrison numbers were reduced somewhat and most of the barracks were demolished to make way for stone granaries. The fort became a supply base for Hadrian's Wall in Wallsend, four miles to the east, for the campaigns of Emperor Septimus Severus in AD 208–210.

In the early fourth century the fort was attacked and burnt down, but it was quickly rebuilt. Close to the end of the Roman rule a squadron of Syrian bargemen from the Tigris were garrisoned here, they gave the fort the name it is known by today – Arbeia; meaning 'Fort of the Arab troops'. The Romans had previously called it Lugudunum. The unit occupied Arbeia until the Romans left Britain in the early fifth century.

The site was occupied well into the eleventh century by the Anglo-Saxons, and then left deserted. The remaining buildings were demolished and the land was used for farming until, in 1875, the first archaeological excavations of the Roman fort began. Digging on the site of the headquarters building immediately proved successful with a complete column being uncovered, as well as engraved gemstones and coins. A decorated tombstone of Regina was revealed in remarkable condition. She was a British woman of the Cattivellauni tribe, who was a slave, and then a freewoman. She was the wife of Barates, a Syrian merchant who added a message of mourning in his native Aramaic on her tombstone. Further digs in 1949–50 by Ian Richmond discovered the perimeter boundaries, and a museum was opened in 1953. Excavations continue to this day and the museum is managed, and the site cared for, by Tyne and Wear Museums. Some gruesome discoveries have been made in recent years; two adolescent skeletons dating back to the fifth century

The reconstructed West Gate at Arbeia. (By kind permission of Tyne and Wear Museums)

with deep cuts in their skulls were revealed in a pit in the centre of the courtyard. A large number of human remains have also been found in one area, leading many to believe that Arbeia might have been the site of one of the largest Roman burial grounds in the north.

The West Gate, the barracks, and the Commanding Officer's house have been reconstructed on their original foundations, based on the detailed evidence available, and gives visitors a chance to experience the magnificence of Roman architecture, and how life in Roman times would have been. The museum contains a variety of exhibits including inscriptions, tombstones, and a recreation of a Roman burial. There is also an array of weaponry, including a welded iron sword with a brass inlay showing Mars, the Roman god of war.

With over 5,000 years of history, it comes as little surprise that there have been numerous ghost sightings at Arbeia. It is reported that locals have seen soldiers in full Roman garb walking throughout the ruined remains of the fort, often walking past a building or a pillar, then vanishing. One witness claims to have been passing late one night and saw a ghostly Roman soldier standing in front of the reconstructed West Gate. As they looked closer they realised, to their horror, that the soldier appeared to be a skeleton. A skull peeped out from beneath the helmet with gaping eye sockets and a loose jaw. Skeletal hands grasped a shield and a short sword. They were absolutely terrified and looked around in the street for someone, anyone, to come over and see this for themselves. The streets were deserted, they were on their own. When they looked back the skeletal warrior was no longer there.

The excavated site of Arbeia Roman fort. (By kind permission of Tyne and Wear Museums)

The original site of Arbeia was much larger than the excavated site today, resulting in many of the current houses nearby standing on the foundations of the Roman buildings. The cellar of the nearby Look Out public house stands on the same level as the original fort, and staff members of the pub have reported seeing Roman soldiers marching through the cellar before walking into a wall.

Darren Ritson, author of *Ghost Hunter: True-Life Encounters from the North East*, and co-author of *The South Shields Poltergeist: One Family's Fight Against an Invisible Intruder*, conducted a paranormal investigation at Arbeia and took the time to tell me what happened:

I went to Arbeia during the day for a pre-investigation visit and experienced, what I believe, to be a paranormal occurrence. I was in the Commanding Officer's quarters and I tried to take a photo with my digital camera. I pressed the button but nothing happened, I tried again but to no avail, so I used my Nikon SLR 35mm and pointed it, clicked, and again nothing. I lowered the camera towards the floor to see what the problem was and it went off. One camera malfunctioning is not unusual, but two? I believe that there was a presence with me and it did not want his or her photo taken.

Early into the investigation that night a blue flashing light was seen in the Commanding Officer's house, a few minutes later it was seen again. The atmosphere then seemed to change as if we were not alone; the temperature dropped and the air around us became ice-cold, resulting in goose bumps. We headed to a section of the house where three bedrooms are joined by a corridor. I had previously locked the door of the corridor, witnessed by two other investigators, but when I went to open the door it was already unlocked.

Later we went to the Great Hall to check on a trigger object, an item which we place onto a piece of paper and draw around so we can tell if it is moved, which we had left in a locked room. As with the door in the Commanding Officer's house, I had locked it in the presence of two other people, but again this door was now unlocked! When we went into the room the trigger object had been moved too. We later found a third locked door had been mysteriously unlocked. We discussed the unlocked doors with the staff at Arbeia after the investigation, and we were told that this was not the first instance of this happening. Staff had previously reported doors in the Commanding Officer's house unlocking of their own volition.

Visitor Information

Address:
Arbeia Roman Fort and Museum
Baring Street
South Shields
NE33 2BB

Tel: 0191 2326789
Website: www.twmuseums.org.uk/arbeia

Opening Hours: 1 April–31 October, Monday–Saturday 10 a.m.–5.30 p.m., Sunday 1 p.m.–5 p.m.; 1 November–31 March, Monday–Saturday 10 a.m.–3.30 p.m. Closed Sunday.
Closed 25 and 26 December and 1 January

How to Get There: Arbeia Roman Fort is situated on Baring Street, in South Shields

Additional Information:
- There is access for wheelchair users via ramp
- There are toilet facitilies, including a disabled toilet
- Facilities for deaf and hard of hearing visitors
- Hot and cold drinks on sale
- Gift shop
- Picnic area

Arts Centre Washington

*T*he Arts Centre Washington is on the site of a medieval farm, with many of the historic farm buildings incorporated into the modern centre, offering a gallery, artist's studios, rehearsal rooms, a fully licensed bar, a recording studio, function rooms, and a theatre. It was in the room now used as a theatre that a suicide took place many years ago. A woman hung herself from a beam, and it is this same woman that is believed to haunt the theatre to this day; a dark shadow is often seen sat at the back of the auditorium. Staff have seen figures walking up the main staircase, and also through a wall which stands where a previous staircase once stood. Bar staff and customers have experienced unusual happenings; with bottles being thrown from shelves, the radio changing frequency on it's own, and the smell of roses being inexplicably reported on numerous occasions. In the 1990s residents in the area made a series of formal complains about loud noises coming from the centre late into the night. However, the centre was locked up, and empty, on each of these occasions.

In July 1994, the arts centre held a display of coin-operated puppets, each puppet would perform a novel action when money was inserted, and one of the puppets was fitted with a Polaroid camera that would take a photograph which it would dispense a few moments later. The morning after the puppets were initially set up, staff turning up for work were astounded to discover that the camera had been activated during the night and a photograph dispensed. No money had been put into the puppet, and the building had been empty. The mystery deepened, and blood ran cold, when the staff looked at the photograph and could all clearly see a misty woman with long blonde hair staring directly into the camera.

I spent an afternoon with Carole Chipchase, Pauline Haughey, and Paul Stothard who have all worked at the Arts Centre Washington for a number of years. Pauline began by telling me of the things that she, and the other staff have experienced at the centre.

We have had a lot of unusual occurrences. Electrical appliances often turn themselves on and off, including lights and radios. There was a period where the photocopier would turn itself off whenever anyone went to use it. One day I was using the

Arts Centre Washington. (By kind permission of Arts Centre Washington)

The theatre; the most active room in the centre. (By kind permission of Arts Centre Washington)

photocopier and I pressed the start button and it turned itself off, but when I tried to turn it back on I found it had been turned off at the wall socket behind the photocopier. I was the only person in the room.

A few years ago there was a medium here late one night. We took him into the theatre and he walked up and down the row of seats, then stopped suddenly. He closed his eyes and started to breath deeply as if in a trance. He then said, 'who's this young person?' and at that precise moment the large door swung open and then slammed shut.

A class came from a school in Biddick to do a workshop, and all the pupils wanted to know about the ghosts. So we were in the theatre and the kids were all engrossed in the stories of things that had happened. When we left the theatre the teacher had forgotten something so went back into the theatre alone. She came running out as white as a sheet, terrified. She took the pupils straight back to the school and would not talk to anyone about what had happened to her in the theatre.

When we were having a lot of rewiring done we had an electrician in the theatre alone, and he was stood on some scaffolding. He had a feeling there was someone at the bottom of it and he looked down, there was no one there. A few moments later the scaffolding starting shaking, he ran out and refused to go back in.

Paul told me of more supernatural occurrences to take place at Arts Centre Washington:

We have a craft fair on the first Saturday of every month, and one week a lady stallholder collapsed and died. A few weeks later I was locking up at night, I'd checked all the rooms were empty and went out to my taxi. The taxi driver said that just before I came out a woman had walked into the centre. I asked what she looked like and he described her as short with a black top and black skirt on. I went back in and checked all the rooms and there was no one in the building. When I got back in the taxi I asked the driver to describe the woman again, in as much detail as he could. His description matched the woman who has died at the craft fair perfectly.

There was a drug-awareness production staged here in the theatre. A girl on stage stopped suddenly as she saw a man appear on stage alongside her. He was wearing an old-fashioned army uniform. Terrified, she ran off the stage, and when she dared to look back she saw him walk through a wall. A number of people have claimed to see this man; it is believed he dates back to the period when the centre was used as a farm, and that he was having an affair with the farmer's wife.

One year, after a New Year's party, we came upstairs and decided to carry out an experiment with a Ouija board. We sat down around a table and as we all touched the glass the alarm started going off. However, as soon as we took our fingers off the glass the alarm stopped. The alarm cannot be reset in the centre, an engineer has to be called out to do it, so there was no way that someone could have been playing a practical joke.

On another occasion, the centre's alarm went off in the middle of the night for no apparent reason. The engineer who came out to reset it brought a big German Shepherd dog with him, and as he entered the arts centre the dog refused to come into the building. All of its fur stood up and it started to growl and bark very aggressively into the darkened doorway.

Visitor Information

Address:
Arts Centre Washington
Biddick Lane
Fatfield
Washington
Tyne and Wear
NE38 8AB

Tel: 0191 2193455
Website: www.artscentrewashington.com
Email: Matthew.Blyth@sunderland.gov.uk

Opening Hours: Please check the website, or contact the centre for opening times and forthcoming events

How to Get There: Washington is signposted from the A1 or the A19 south of Newcastle, join the A1231 Washington Highway and follow signs for Fatfield

Additional Information:
- The centre holds a monthly craft fair on the first Saturday of every month from 10 a.m. You can purchase a range of hand-made goods, from ceramics and glass-ware to jewellery and textiles
- The Courtyard café/bar is open regular pub hours and offers the visitor a good value meal for lunch or dinner. For further details please ring 0191 2193463 or email: thecourtyardbar@aol.com
- Arts Centre Washington is available for parties and conferences with a range of function suites

Bessie Surtees House

*B*essie Surtees was the daughter of wealthy merchant, and mayor of Newcastle, Aubone Surtees. In 1771, seventeen-year-old Bessie fell in love with a Scotsman, twenty-two-year-old John Scott, an Oxford tutor and the son of William Scott, a coal merchant. The Scotts were not social equals to the Surtees, and Aubone forbid Bessie to see John again. She was made to live in the south of England for a while in the hope that it would make her see that he was not the man for her. Aubone had already picked a suitor for his daughter, a man named Sir Walter Blackett, an MP for forty years and he had been mayor of Newcastle five times. He was fifty years older than Bessie, but Aubone believed that Bessie would understand that marrying Blackett would ensure she enjoyed the best things in life, and would make the Surtees family even richer and more powerful.

When Bessie returned to the north, Aubone believed she had taken his advice on board and had no further contact with John Scott. This was not the case however; when she was going for her morning ride she was meeting him in secret on Shields Road. Bessie had told him of her father's plan of marriage to Sir Walter Blackett, so John Scott concocted a plan. He asked Bessie to run away to Scotland with him, where they could legally wed without her parents' permission. On the night of 18 November 1772, Bessie climbed out of her window and down a ladder into John's arms. They hurried to Blackshiels, a village near Dalkieth where they were married. Shortly afterwards they returned to Newcastle, and were welcomed by John's mother and father who invited them to live in their house on Love Lane. Aubone Surtees was not so forgiving. He disowned Bessie, believing her to have ruined her own life, and turned him into a laughing stock. After several weeks, however, his anger subsided and he began to spend time with his daughter again, he also began to accept John as his son-in-law. With the blessing of her father, Bessie and John had an English wedding at St Nicholas' Church on 19 January 1773 with both sets of parents in attendance.

The house that Bessie and her parents lived in on Newcastle's quayside still stands today as a rare example of well-preserved domestic architecture from the Jacobean period. It stands five stories high, with each floor slightly overhanging the one below, and the windows extending across the full width of the house. The interior is decorated in grand oak panelling and elaborate plaster ceilings.

Bessie's spirit is believed to remain in the house and it is said that she can be seen peering through the first-floor window, as she would have done while waiting for her lover on the fateful night that they ran away to Scotland.

The interior of the house. The window to the far right is the one through which Bessie climbed to elope with John Scott. It is identifiable by a blue pane of glass.
(By kind permission of English Heritage)

Bessie Surtees House. (By kind permission of English Heritage)

Visitor Information

Address:
Bessie Surtees House
41–44 Sandhill
Newcastle-upon-Tyne
NE1 3JF

Tel: 0191 2691200
Website: www.english-heritage.org.uk

Opening Hours: Monday–Friday 10 a.m.–4 p.m.
Closed 24 December–5 January and bank holidays

How to Get There: Bessie Surtees House is found on Newcastle's quayside

Additional Information:
- Dogs are not allowed
- There is a shop
- There are toilets

The Blackie Boy

*T*he Blackie Boy, situated in the Groat Market, is one of the oldest public houses in Newcastle and is a popular drinking spot, especially at the weekend.

The Blackie Boy can be a creepy place, especially when it's quiet, or late in the evening after the last customer has left and the doors have been closed. For a number of years customers and members of staff have reported unusual happenings and an eerie feeling of being watched. A male member of staff was once changing a light bulb in a toilet on the second floor when a woman's voice suddenly called out from one of the cubicles, 'What are you doing in here?' The shaken man knew that he was the only person in there and he hesitated. Suddenly the woman's voice screamed out from the empty cubicle, 'Get out! Get out!' The terrified man couldn't get out fast enough, his heart racing. A colleague came from downstairs to see what all of the noise was. The two of them returned to the toilets to find it completely empty and that the screaming had stopped.

The assistant manager of the Blackie Boy, Steven Hickman, told me of some his experiences within the haunted pub.

One evening a medium came to the Blackie Boy and I set up a camera on the first floor, and sat completely alone. I called out asking if anyone was there and at that precise moment an orb appeared and floated past the camera. I ran downstairs, terrified not even thinking to pick up my torch or turn the light on. I've not been back upstairs alone since.

It's fairly common for the toilet doors in the second floor function room to suddenly swing open violently, or slam shut. They are heavy doors and could not be moved by a draft.

The Blackie Boy.

Visitor Information

Address:
The Blackie Boy
11 Groat Market
Newcastle-upon-Tyne
NE1 1UQ

Tel: 0191 2320730

Opening Hours: Monday–Saturday 11 a.m.–11 p.m., Sunday midday–10.30 p.m.

How to Get There: The Blackie Boy is found in the Groat Market, in the Bigg Market in the centre of Newcastle-upon-Tyne

Additional Information:
- The upstairs function room is available for parties for up to 100 people with champagne and canapés available on request. For more information contact the Blackie Boy
- From the alley to the right-hand side of the bar you can access Perdu, the sister bar to the Blackie Boy

The Blacksmith's Table

The Blacksmith's Table is one of the oldest buildings in Washington village, believed to be around 400 years old. It was opened as a blacksmith's to service the Old Hall Estate. Since it was a commercial building it didn't feature on census, making it incredibly difficult to date the building accurately. However, it did appear on the first ever map of Washington in the late eighteenth century.

The building was used as the village smithy until 1954, the last blacksmith's being the Dobson family. From 1954, it was opened as a variety of businesses, including a pottery run by David Gibson, which closed down in 1984. Between 1984 and 1987 the building lay empty, and the fabric of the building began to deteriorate and had been badly vandalised. In 1987, the present owner, Paul Cajiao bought the building and set about turning it into a restaurant with his wife Pam. The Blacksmith's Table opened its doors on 20 May 1988 and it remains a popular restaurant today.

The building is home to a number of spirits including a blacksmith who sits at table 9 with his elbows on his knees taking a keen interest in what happens within 'his' building. A white lady has been seen, often walking through a wall which was once a doorway, it is believed that she may be the ghost of Jane Atkinson who was ducked to death in 1676 for being a witch. She lost her life in the village pond which used to be at the front of the building. A man sits at table 6, his head resting on his hand, watching people coming and going. There's also a man who stands next to the front door staring at a wall, occasionally looking over his shoulder, but never moving.

The most famous of the Blacksmith's Table's ghosts is that of Robert Hazlitt. He was a highwayman who robbed in an area known as Gateshead Fell, a remote stretch of land including an area of Wrekenton, called the Long Bank. Hazlitt robbed a mail coach here in 1770, and this was witnessed by a local post-boy. A few days later Hazlitt was in Washington having his horse shod at the village smithy. The post-boy was in Washington and spotted Hazlitt's distinctive horse, he rushed to the local Justice of the Peace. The Justice of the Peace and the post-boy went to the blacksmith's, and the smithy explained that the man was a good customer and had left his horse with him and was going to return later to pick it up. When Hazlitt returned he was arrested and taken away to face trial. As he was dragged away, he cursed the blacksmith for aiding his capture. Robert Hazlitt was hanged

The Blacksmith's Table at night. (By kind permission of the Blacksmith's Table)

in Durham and his body was hung in a gibbet cage in Wrekenton as a warning to other would-be highwaymen.

The ghost of Robert Hazlitt is often seen in the bar area of the Blacksmith's Table, this would have been the area that horses were tied to the hitching rail which is still present in the bar today. Whenever Hazlitt's ghostly form is seen, he is only seen from the shins up, this is likely to be due to the original floor level in 1770 being lower than what it is today.

I visited the Blacksmith's Table late one night in September 2008 and spent some time in the company of Paul Cajiao, who told me of the building's ghostly residents:

When we first took over the building we began to experience odd things. My wife and I are both very spiritual people and we went to a spiritualist church and got a number of messages from the ghosts that haunt the Blacksmith's Table.

We've had lots of customers experience things, we had one couple who were here in September, and it was his birthday. They had been here on exactly the same date last year, sitting at the same table, and they told us that when they were here last year they both saw a woman walk down through the restaurant and then turn left and walk through the wall. They said they hadn't said anything last year as they'd felt a bit embarrassed by it.

We've had a report of something here tonight, we've had a couple at table 11 who are spiritualists and the husband was telling me that as they were eating something touched him. He asked the spirit to leave them alone as they were trying to eat and he didn't experience anything else.

We don't go looking for the ghosts that reside here, we've been here for twenty years now and we just accept that they are here. Things happen so often that we've probably forgotten more stories than we can remember.

One medium picked up on a former blacksmith who sits at table nine at the back corner of the restaurant, and he said to us, through the medium, that he is very pleased to see that we are continuing his work in his building. We thought this was strange because, of course, we're not blacksmiths so we wondered what was meant by this. The medium took Pat's hand and put a symbolic key into her hand, as requested by the blacksmith, and closed her fingers over it.

We later made further enquiries and we found out that back in the old days, most villages would have its own blacksmith, and the blacksmith's building was always a warm place because of the work that was done there. Men would go out into the fields, and after work people would congregate in the smithy as it was nice and warm, it was like the community centre of its day. So it appears the message the blacksmith passed on to us was because his building was a social place, a place where people went and enjoyed themselves, and this is what happens here on a daily basis now. This is the kind of experience which is very important to us, getting a personal message like that is a wonderful thing.

We had a ghost hunting group investigate a few years back, and it was around 1 a.m. and we were sat around table seven and we joined hands. One of the female members of the team claimed to be a medium and after a short while she appeared to become possessed. Suddenly this big booming male voice came out of her and shouted 'It wasn't me, I didn't do it. I'm innocent' and repeated this over and over. Then she came out with a name, I can't remember exactly what it was, but it was not a name that I'd ever heard associated with this building before. The obvious name for her to pick up on would, of course, have been Robert Hazlitt, the ghost that everyone associates with the Blacksmith's Table. This girl had been possessed for a while and the rest of her team, including her boyfriend, were terrified, and becoming increasingly worried about her, so they tried to bring her out of the trance. The evening ended and we thought nothing more of it, the name the girl had came out with was interesting, but it was not a name we'd heard before so didn't seem overly impressive.

A couple of years later I bumped into to a local lady who was very keen on history, and she told me that she'd been doing some research into Washington, and into the Blacksmith's Table. We got chatting and she said, 'Did you know that Robert Hazlitt wasn't his real name?' I asked what she meant, and she went onto explain that Robert Hazlitt had been one of his aliases, in the same way that the most famous highwaymen of them all, Dick Turpin, had also used the name John Palmer. Robert Hazlitt's real name was in fact the name that the medium at the ghost hunt had come out with while she appeared to be possessed by Hazlitt. When you get some information like that over the space of two years, and the people are not connected, that's very interesting and further proof of Hazlitt's ghost remaining here.

When we first opened the building as a restaurant I had a local artist paint the scene of a highwayman being arrested here, in the old smithy. I was really pleased with it and hung it in the bar, where it remains to this day. The week I hung it up, we had an incredibly good week for no apparent reason. Whether it was coincidence, or whether it was in some way Robert Hazlitt repaying us to show that he approves of the painting we'll never know. Every year on the anniversary of the Blacksmith's Table we have a party, and every year I always make a speech, and at the end of my speech we drink a toast to Robert Hazlitt and the other spirits that call this building their home. People have asked why we don't get the building exorcised, but who are we to do something like that? They were here before we arrived, and they'll be here for a long time after we're gone. They don't cause us any problems and they seem to have accepted us in the same way we've accepted them.

Visitor Information

Address:
The Blacksmith's Table
The Green
Washington Village
Tyne and Wear
NE38 7AB

Tel: 0191 4151788
Website: www.blacksmithstable.com

Opening Hours: Tuesday–Friday 5.30 p.m.–10 p.m. (5.30 p.m.–7 p.m. by advance booking only), Saturday 6.30 p.m.–10 p.m., Sunday lunch 1 p.m.–2.30 p.m.
All times are flexible upon specific request

How to Get There: From the A1 or A19, join the A1231, then follow the signs for Washington Old Hall, the Blacksmith's Table is opposite

Additional Information:
- The Blacksmith's Table's menu can be found on their website. However, due to seasonal items and culinary trends please call the Blacksmith's Table for full details of their current menu
- Throughout the year the Blacksmith's Table offers a variety of special events to supplement their regular services, such as live music and wine-tasting dinners. Please check the forthcoming events page of their website for further details
- The Blacksmith's Table caters for a range of corporate events, such as company presentations, seminars, sales meetings, business meetings, staff training, exhibitions, and corporate hospitality
- The Blacksmith's Table provides the perfect setting for wedding receptions and private functions of all types. The restaurant is capable of comfortably seating forty people. Special menus are individually prepared to clients' personal requirements

Bowes Railway and National Heritage Museum

*T*he original railway at Springwell, Sunderland, was opened in 1826, and was built by George Stephenson, the famed railroad engineer and inventor of the *Rocket*, the most famous of the early railway locomotives. Due to a new colliery being opened in Springwell, a railway was required to transport coal to the River Tyne via the Jarrow Stathes. Stephenson designed the railway to function by utilising a combination of inclines relying on gravity, and steam-engine technology. The line was soon extended to serve a number of other collieries to a length of fifteen miles.

In 1932 the company was rebranded the Bowes Railway, after John Bowes, one of the companies senior partners and a big name in the coal trade in the north. In 1947, the Bowes Railway became part of the National Coal Board and a substantial sum of money was invested into the modernisation of the line.

In the 1960s hundreds of north-east coal mines were closed and as a result the railway line was cut back, and in 1974 closed down altogether.

In 1976 a group of enthusiasts took over the line and received government backing to re-open Bowes Railway, the only surviving standard gauge rope-hauled railway in the world, as a museum. The railway line from Bankfell Bank Head to Springwell has been restored to working condition, as have a large number of the original buildings, the oldest of which are the joiner's and blacksmith's shops, which date back to the railway's opening in 1826. The museum is also home to a number of steam locomotives and trucks rescued from the old colliery railways. Many have been restored and are in working condition, and on special open days can be seen in action.

The railway, and the colliery, saw a great number of accidents and deaths during the working life of the site. One of the restored features of the museum is the Blackham's Hill hauler house and it's rope-worked incline system. This system was a pulley which would move at a rapid speed, safety standards were low and workers would occasionally get caught in the rope as it moved and would be literaly torn in two.

The colliery suffered explosions in 1833, 1837 and 1869, killing hundreds of men and children, some as young as eight, and seriously injuring and maiming many more.

The Colliery Courtyard. Surrounded by workshops, this area would be used for the repair and construction of wagons. (By kind permission of Bowes Railway and National Heritage Museum)

It is also believed that in more recent years there was a suicide at the railway. There has been so much loss of life at Bowes Railway, that it seems the site has became a hotbed of paranormal activity.

A ghostly man, wearing a flat cap and overalls, has been seen in the engineering room. He crosses the room; always retracing the exact same path, then vanishes. Footsteps have been heard on the gravel path outside the workshops, when a member of staff has gone to check there has been no one there. A strange smell of soap has been experienced in the blacksmith's shop, and children's laughter has been heard in the workshops.

Jay Brown, of Northern Ghost Investigations has spent several nights at Bowes Railway Museum as part of organised ghost hunts and told me of some of the inexplicable happenings that he has experienced:

> Northern Ghost Investigations have made a few visits to Bowes Railway Museum over the years and it has always been an interesting time – although, our very first visit to the museum was by far the most active. There are two incidents which have stuck in my mind since.

Bowes Railway and National Heritage Museum; to the back right of the photograph is Blackham's Hill hauler house. Many people lost their lives being accidentally caught in the wheel which operated this rope-worked incline system. (By kind permission of Bowes Railway and National Heritage Museum)

The first incident was in the blacksmith's shop at the bottom end of the museum. We'd heard a couple of tales surrounding this location from the caretaker of the museum, one of which concerned stories of previous visitors running from the room screaming! So I for one was looking forward to my time spent in there. Sadly, nothing happened and the location seemed as dead as the proverbial to me, which was a little disappointing.

However, later that night, a small group, including myself, were in the area of the blacksmith's shop investigating another location within the museum. Suddenly, I heard a noise from behind the door of the blacksmith's shop that sounded like metal striking metal. Our small group were the only people at this end of the museum and I knew nobody else other than those I could visibly account for were present.

Not thinking much of it, I casually made my way to the blacksmith's shop to investigate – maybe somebody had slipped in without me noticing? It was worth taking a look if nothing else.

I managed to get approximately 10ft from the door when I seemed to walk into – *something*. The best way I can describe it was a wall of energy that seemed to not want me to approach the door, I was genuinely afraid of going any further. I'd never experienced such raw fear like that before on an investigation or even since – I was seriously spooked. I felt as though some force emanating from the blacksmith's shop did not want me to approach the door.

Being an intrepid investigator, I did the only sensible thing one would do – I called out to the other three in this small group to head over to where I was to give me a little moral support! When our small group gathered, each of the others immediately felt what I was experiencing and described exactly the same thing I was feeling at exactly the same spot I had stopped at.

Gingerly we approached the door. Although strengthened by the others with me, each step seemed to get harder and harder and the sense of foreboding grew. We got to the door and slowly pushed it open. The room was empty – but the sense of a strong presence in the blacksmith's shop remained.

Something did not want us in that room and was using the sheer force of its presence to get us to leave. But we didn't. We stood in the open doorway just watching and waiting. I called out, asking whoever was present to show themselves but nobody did. Over the course of the next few minutes, we felt the sense of dread slowly fade as whatever it was must have decided to leave itself.

If it was this presence that had caused previous groups to run screaming from the blacksmith's shop – then I can perfectly understand why.

Our second interesting incident occurred later in the night whilst in the joiner's shop. Our small group had dotted themselves around and had spent forty minutes or so there, almost bored with the lack of anything remotely interesting within the location.

Upstairs, in a display room situated within an old storage area, another small group seemed to be having just as quiet a time as we were.

I'd positioned myself on the metal staircase and was calling out to anything present or merely passing by, to try and make contact with us. A sensitive with us claimed that a spirit – a man – was present in the joiner's shop, standing in a corner watching us in an almost amused manner. But no matter how we much tried they didn't seem interested in 'performing any tricks' for us, as we were told by the sensitive.

Admittedly, I was getting a little frustrated which I know I shouldn't. After the earlier incident in the blacksmith's shop I was determined to make some sort of contact with any entities present within the museum.

I don't normally feel frustrated on an investigation but I felt that games were being played. Other groups during the night had felt the same too – something seemed to be teasing us, just drawing us in and then leaving us right at the edge and was seemingly taking pleasure from it. I think the frustration I was feeling was becoming evident in my voice as I was calling out.

The Joiner's Shop; one of the oldest remaining buildings of the original railway. (By kind permission of Bowes Railway and National Heritage Museum)

At one point, the sensitive claimed that she had just been told by the spirit in the corner that I should 'shut up'. I never did, of course, and continued calling out trying to get something from the man. Again, the sensitive said 'shut up'. It would appear that the man was getting riled. Normally, I would ease off at this point as I don't want to upset anybody – dead or alive – but the frustration I was feeling was seemingly getting a life of its own.

'He's shouting now Jay – shut up, shut up – over and over again', the sensitive told me but onwards I pushed.

Suddenly, I saw something move fast in the corner of my eye and I instinctively raised my arm to protect myself. I didn't need to as whatever it was seemed to miss me and clattered noisily on the metal staircase eliciting screams and shouts from both downstairs in the joiner's shop where we were and upstairs in the display room.

Upon investigation, we found a large piece of wood – some six inches long resting on one of the stairs. Alarmingly, it had been cut in a way that one of the corners came to a sharp point that would cause serious damage if someone had been hit by it – and certainly with the force it seemingly had been thrown.

Visitor Information

Address:
Bowes Railway and National Heritage Museum
Springwell Village
Gateshead
Tyne and Wear
NE9 7QJ

Tel: 0191 4161847
Website: www.bowesrailway.co.uk

Opening Hours: The site is open Monday–Friday 10 a.m.–3 p.m. all year.
Trains operate on selected Sundays and open days advertised on the Bowes Railway website

How to Get There: From the Washington Highway A1231, follow the signs for Gateshead/Newcastle and at the roundabout leading onto the A1, take the third exit onto the B1288 and follow the signs for Bowes Railway

Additional Information:
- A number of special events and open days take place at Bowes Railway each year. Please visit the website for further information. The museum is also available to arrange bespoke events if required
- Bowes Railway is continuously seeking volunteers to help out at the site; there is further information on the museum's website
- Please note there are no toilet facilities at the museum
- The railway is not suitable for visitors in wheelchairs
- Please note there is no gift shop, nor are there refreshments on sale

The Carriage

The Carriage public house started life as Jesmond railway station, originally built in 1864. The station was in use for over 100 years until it was closed in 1977 when the Metro system was introduced. It was converted into a pub in 1981 and paranormal occurrences have been reported throughout the building ever since.

The most commonly reported phenomenon by staff and customers is the feeling that someone is standing behind them waiting to get past. Upon moving out of the way to let them pass, there's no one there, although some people have seen a grey mist move past them before disappearing.

Poltergeist activity is commonplace, with glasses being thrown from the bar, always landing upright and never breaking. However, some of the poltergeist phenomena has been much more violent; a member of the owner's family was washing up in the kitchen when a fish slice flew across the room striking him in the chest, this was quickly followed by a ladle.

Liz Harrison, manager of the Carriage, told me of an inexplicable occurrence at the Carriage on the night of Hallowe'en 2008, leaving one customer bruised and bloodied:

The Carriage.

Every Hallowe'en we do the pub up with spooky decorations and banners, and a life-size skeleton hanging above the bar. The regulars often join in the spirit of things by turning up for our annual Hallowe'en quiz in fancy dress. During the quiz this year the question was asked, 'what do you call a spirit which moves objects around?' At that precise moment a plate fell from a bookcase striking the female customer sitting below cutting her on the head. The plate had been there for years and never moved, perhaps our ghost was just trying to give the quiz participants a clue? It couldn't have been timed better.

The unusual happenings at the Carriage have been attributed to the tragic death of two passengers that were standing on the old station platform when a bomb struck during the Second World War.

Visitor Information

Address:
The Carriage
Old Jesmond Station
Archibold Terrace
Jesmond
Newcastle-upon-Tyne
NE2 1DB

Tel: 0191 2818382

Opening Hours: Monday–Saturday 11.30 a.m.–11 p.m., Sunday midday–10.30 p.m.

How to Get There: From the Coast Road, A1058, follow the signs for City Centre onto Osbourne Terrace, B1307, then follow signs onto A1057. From Newcastle city centre the Carriage is found close to Jesmond Metro station, close to Northumbria University, a ten minute walk from the Haymarket in the centre of Newcastle.

Additional Information:
• There is a railway carriage attached to the pub which has been converted into an Indian restaurant named Valley Junction 397
• An evening menu is available with bar meals, burgers and rolls from 7 p.m. Toasted sandwiches are also served 2.30 p.m.–10 p.m. Sunday Lunch is served midday–2.30 p.m. A takeaway service is available by contacting 0191 2812151
• Every Sunday night is jazz night
• Children are welcome

The Castle Garth

*I*n AD 120 the Romans built the first bridge to cross the River Tyne. They named the bridge '*Pons Aelius*', meaning 'Bridge of Aelius', Aelius being the family name of the Emperor Hadrian (who was responsible for the Roman wall built in AD 122 from Segedunum at Wallsend to the shore of the Solway Firth). The Romans also built a fort overlooking the Tyne to protect the crossing.

During the eighth century, the settlement came to be known as Monkchester, and the site of the now ruined Roman fort was used as a Christian cemetery and a monastery.

In 1080, Robert Curthose, eldest son of William the Conqueror, founded a castle in Monkchester, which became known as *Novum Castellum*, meaning 'New Castle'. It was a motte-and-bailey construction on the site of the cemetery, the building of which disturbed hundreds of graves when the foundations were being dug. The fortified castle was enclosed within a clay rampart, topped with a wooden palisade, and surrounded by an external ditch.

Between 1168 and 1178, King Henry I ordered that the castle be rebuilt in stone at a cost of £1,144 5s 6d. A rectangular stone keep was built, and a triangular stone bailey was built to replace the existing wooden one. During the construction William 'the Lion' of Scotland led an invasion, but was captured and held in the castle. Evidence of this interruption is present to this very day, with a fifteen-step staircase coming to an abrupt stop against a wall on the second floor of the castle's keep.

The castle's barbican, a fortified gateway, was built between 1247 and 1250. It would later be known as the Black Gate, named after wealthy London merchant Patrick Black who leased the gatehouse in the seventeenth century. Work began on the town walls in 1272 to repel Scottish invaders; when they were complete the walls were almost two miles long, and two metres thick.

In 1296 William Wallace led the Scottish army south, destroying Corbridge, but avoiding the heavily defended Newcastle. The following year Wallace, alongside Andrew de Moray, led the Scots to victory over the English at the Battle of Stirling Bridge. Wallace and de Moray then marched the Scottish army south, almost reaching Newcastle but turning away and heading to Carlisle instead. In 1305, William Wallace was executed in London. It was a horrific death. He was hung, drawn and quartered – strangled by hanging but released while still alive,

The Castle Keep. (By kind permission of the Society of Antiquaries)

The Black Gate. (By kind permission of the Society of Antiquaries)

emasculated, eviscerated, and his bowels and intestines burnt before his eyes, beheaded, then cut into four parts. His right arm-quarter was displayed on the bridge at Newcastle, with a number of his internal organs, and other unnamed pieces of his anatomy being displayed on the walls of the keep.

In 1323, Andrew de Harcla, the 1st Earl of Carlisle was executed for treason, and in another bloody display, one of his quarters was placed upon on the castle walls.

In the year 1400 Newcastle became a town and county, separated from the jurisdiction of Northumberland. This was granted by Henry IV at the request of Roger Thornton, the mayor of Newcastle. However, the Castle Garth and its land remained part of Northumberland. Due to the changing political situation, the strategic importance of the castle had declined, and the Castle Keep became Northumberland's county gaol. Newcastle's gaol was at Newgate, within the town wall. Criminals wanted for offences within Newcastle simply took up sanctuary within the castle walls, therefore technically within the county of Northumberland and safe from being brought to justice, despite being separated from the county of Newcastle by only a few feet.

The conditions for prisoners held at the Castle Keep were horrendous. Due to being overcrowded, petty thieves, most often children, would be thrown into cells

The Garrison Room. (By kind permission of the Society of Antiquaries)

with murderers. The thieves often would lose their lives within that cell at the hands of the convicted killers. There was no segregation, men and women being imprisoned together, resulting in a large number of women and girls in their early teens being raped by the male prisoners. Disease was rife, due to the conditions that prisoners lived in; amongst rats and human waste. The number of people who died of illness while being held at the Castle Keep would have run well into the hundreds.

Another grisly public display on the Castle Keep's walls took place in 1415 when a quarter of Harry Hotspur was placed there after his execution for the Percy family's part in the rebellion against Henry IV.

In 1589 Queen Elizabeth granted the Newcastle authorities permission to cross into the castle grounds and arrest criminals taking refuge. By this point in time the upkeep of the Castle Keep had been neglected for over 200 years and had begun to fall into disrepair, the walls were beginning to crumble and the keep no longer had a roof. The prisoners being held there could be living in up to six inches of water in the winter months.

In 1593, Edward Waterson attempted to escape from Newgate Gaol by burning down his cell door. He was caught and executed; his head cut off and placed upon a spike outside the Newgate Gaol as a warning to others. His body was cut into three pieces and displayed across the town.

Part of the west curtain wall collapsed in 1620, but in 1638 the castle was partially rebuilt and strengthened as war with the Scots looked likely. The Scots invaded Newcastle in 1640 and occupied the town for a year, leaving in August 1641 after being paid £300,000 by the English government to do so.

The Civil War once again saw Royalist Newcastle under heavy attack from the Parliamentarian Scots in 1644. The castle was defended, bravely but ultimately fell. The town was occupied once more by the Scots until 1647.

Fifteen women found guilty of witchcraft and one man guilty of wizardry were hanged on Newcastle Town Moor in 1650; they spent their last days in the bowels of the Keep in the Garrison Room, shackled to the wall. The rings used to chain these prisoners can still be seen on the central pillar in the room.

In 1685 James II declared that the Castle Garth become part of Newcastle, and therefore subject to the town's bylaws.

On 7 December 1733, a local showman placed an advertisment claiming that he would fly from the top of the Castle Keep. A large crowd gathered to watch this amazing feat. As the time drew closer the showman began to lose his nerve, and decided to strap the wings he had fashioned to his faithful donkey instead. The donkey was pushed over the edge and fell 100ft to the ground. Amazingly the donkey survived, landing on an unfortunate onlooker who died instantly.

By the end of the eighteenth century the castle had fallen further into ruin. Houses had been built within the castle walls, the chapel in the keep was being used as a beer cellar by the landlord of the Three Bulls' Heads, and the Black Gate had became a slum tenement.

The Mezzanine Chamber. (By kind permission of the Society of Antiquaries)

In 1810, the Newcastle Corporation bought the ruined Castle Garth for 600 guineas and began to restore it. By 1813 the Castle Keep had been fully restored and was opened to the public as a tourist attraction. During the rebuilding process there was a tragic accident at the castle. The authorities decided to fire cannon shot from the roof of the keep each day at noon. On the 7 May 1812, Gunner John Robson fired a shot from the cannon. He loaded it up for a second shot, but had forgotten to swab out the bore as he loaded a second cannon ball. The embers within the cannon were still burning and fired the second cannon ball the instant it was placed inside the barrel. It blew Robson's right hand clean off and the force threw him over the side of the keep to his death.

Between 1847 and 1849, a railway was built through the centre of Castle Garth, splitting it in two. It looked likely that the remaining Castle Keep and Black Gate would be demolished until the Society of Antiquaries acquired the remains of the Castle Garth, cleared the surrounding land and employed the services of celebrated Newcastle architect John Dobson to carry out further restoration.

During the Second World War the Garrison Room was used as an air-raid shelter, and the keep roof was used a fire wardens' post and air-raid post.

Archaeological excavations at the castle started in 1960, and were completed in 1992. Evidence of the Roman fort was found, along with the Anglo-Saxon burials in the Christian cemetery. However, there was also evidence of earlier occupation; flint flakes and a stone axe predating the Roman artefacts by up to 700 years were also found.

Steeped in a history of violent deaths, the like of which are far worse than can possibly be imagined, and tortured souls seeing out their remaining days within these walls before they were taken away to be executed, it's not surprising that the oldest surviving building in Newcastle-upon-Tyne – the Castle Keep – is unquestionably one of the most haunted buildings in Tyne and Wear, arguably the entire country.

The Castle Keep's most famous ghost has been nicknamed the Poppy Girl. Legend has it that the Poppy Girl was a fifteen-year-old girl named Briony who sold flowers in the town of Newcastle in the late seventeenth century. She was arrested and thrown into a small cell at the bottom of the Castle Keep, with a group of male prisoners. The men had all been condemned to death and had nothing to lose, so they took turns raping young Briony. Within eight days she was dead, she had died in agony from terrible internal injuries. The men continued having sex with Briony's lifeless body even in death, until it was removed from the cell.

Having died in such horrendous circumstances it appears that Briony has not been able to move on from the Castle Keep and continues to haunt the Garrison Room, believed to be the most active room in the castle, and the small rooms within it, including the one Briony lost her life in, known as the Condemned Cell. Visitors have experienced the sobbing of a young girl, often when they are in the Garrison Room alone. A female's scream has also been heard on a number of occasions. Some people have picked up on the fragrance of flowers,

An unusual photograph of a misty figure taken in the Kings Chamber. (Photograph by Darren Ritson, by kind permission of the Society of Antiquaries)

followed by them suddenly becoming overwhelmed with sadness, on occasions leading to them to weep inexplicably or be overcome by nausea. It is as if visitors are picking up on the horrors that the Garrison Room has witnessed over the last 1,000 years, and are somehow experiencing the emotions of those who have suffered here.

The chapel, a large room occupying the basement underneath the main staircase, which retains its original twelfth-century ornate windows and vaulted ceilings, is another room within the castle that is home to spirits remaining from a bygone age. Chanting has been heard in the chapel by many visitors, some also claim to have seen a monk in a dark robe knelt in prayer.

In the Mezzanine Chamber a white light that has been seen to move around before vanishing into a wall. Dark shadows have also been witnessed on numerous occasions.

Visitors in the Great Hall have been terrified by sudden loud banging within the room. Mists rising from the floor, then swirling around the room before vanishing have been experienced, most often at night, and are usually accompanied by a drastic drop in temperature. In the Great Hall, screams have been heard coming from the gallery which runs around the top of the room. Dark shadows have also been seen moving swiftly along the corridors. In 2002, on one of my many visits to the castle, staff at the keep told me that they have seen a tall man wearing a cloak and a top hat walk across the Great Hall on several occasions.

The Great Hall. (By kind permission of the Society of Antiquaries)

West Yorkshire Paranormal Group investigated the Castle Keep in 2007; Pat Adamswright, who is sensitive to supernatural occurrences, told me of what lurked within the ancient fortress on the night of their visit:

The investigation took place on 17 May, 2008, a beautiful day that was to end in a very cold night, for more reasons than just the weather. The whole group was filled with eager anticipation and by the end of the night we had not been disappointed.

My first experience began on the approach to the Great Hall, on the winding staircase. In my minds eye I was being shown a pair of hands holding sackcloth, in which was nestled a man's 'bits'! This definitely caught my attention. It happened again three or four times while walking around the Great Hall, so it was obviously of some significance. Research has since showed that when William Wallace had been hung, drawn and quartered, pieces of him were shipped all over the country as a deterrent. As well as other parts of his body, his 'unmentionables' were sent to Castle Keep.

Another spirit was also present there, drawing attention to an area higher up. This was someone who had had his right hand blown off in a cannon accident on the roof, also being blown over the parapet and dying in the process.

A series of solo vigils in the Mezzanine Chamber brought about the most unusual phenomena of the night. I was sat in the dark and, although it was obvious there was a spirit present, no direct communication was taking place. I then heard the crackle of the walkie-talkie as though someone was trying to get in touch, but no one had used the other one. Replay of the video tape revealed that the crackle of the radio had been covered up with the loudest bang, resembling a metal gate being banged shut. The sound was not heard by anyone else in the building, least of all me, who showed absolutely no reaction on tape. On revision of all the solo vigils on tape, it became obvious that someone from the spirit world seemed to be treading the path along the right-hand wall, towards the stairs. In fact nearly all the participants reported various movements on the stairs.

The other highlight of the night for me was the Garrison Room. I don't know what I was expecting, but it wasn't what I received, which was the form of a medieval pikeman. He did, indeed, seem a comic character, with his clothes hanging very loosely from his bones and his hand grasping this very tall pike, in relation to his stature. However, when one considers that this soul probably came from the time of a siege, and his death was one of starvation and disease, it loses its comic edge.

We were inundated with photographs showing orbs. We had light anomalies from all areas that we covered, except the chapel, there it was the strong smell of beer that we found intriguing.

All in all it was wonderful experience. So much so that we re-booked immediately, and the next visit is imminent, to cover all the areas we missed first time around.

I also spoke to Jay Brown who spent a night at the Castle Keep in September 2008. He told me of the terrifying entity that he encountered in the galleries:

The galleries are a narrow walkway running high up around the Great Hall of the Castle Keep in Newcastle. With only a few small windows giving light from outside, it is a dark and claustrophobic place, with one corner of the galleries in particular, pitch black and disorientating.

There are numerous tales of activity from the galleries, many of which are reported by different witnesses at different times; such as an eerie mist that sometimes appears, and a dark figure that has been seen and photographed. Footsteps have been heard, following a lone explorer.

Whilst on an investigation of the keep with Northern Ghost Investigations we had two witnesses who claimed to see a dark-robed figure following myself around the galleries.

I had taken a walk on my own around the galleries, to check up on a couple of others who were on the walkway opposite to where I was. When I came upon them, they were ashen-faced, but excited.

They had been standing in one of the balconies that overlooks the Great Hall and at the opposite balcony to where they stood they had watched a person walk by, silhouetted against one of the windows, which they had immediately identified as myself. However, as they continued to watch, another figure floated along the same walkway and again was silhouetted against the window mere seconds after I was. They described the figure as a good foot smaller than myself (I'm 6ft 3in) and dressed in what looked like a black hood and robe.

The Galleries. (By kind permission of the Society of Antiquaries)

A paranormal investigator in the Great Hall in 2003 saw a swirling mist rapidly moving around the room. He took this extraordinary photograph just as the mist appeared to head straight for him. (Photograph by Trevor Brown, by kind permission of the Society of Antiquaries)

I immediately gathered our entire group together and we congregated on one of the spiral staircases that leads downwards from the galleries, and the two witnesses repeated their story to all. It was decided that we should each take turns to wander alone around the perimeter of the galleries listening out for the footsteps hopefully following behind while others watched from a balcony.

As we discussed this plan, a strange feeling of oppression descended upon us. I watched as each person looked at the others around them wondering if what they were feeling was being felt by the others – a definite presence was with us and the atmosphere was charged.

The first explorer set off on their journey around the galleries and instantly, the presence seemed to leave us – had it gone to follow her? When she returned, although she claimed to not hear any footsteps, she did say that she felt that she had been pushed into the wall at one point – a gentle push that made her stumble. The second and third explorer made their journey around the galleries without reporting anything but as the fourth person was about to start, once again that strange feeling descended upon us and then left us as the fourth explorer set of.

Once more, no footsteps were reported when he returned, but he did claim to hear a slapping sound, as though hands were hitting the wall beside where he walked.

There is little doubt that the galleries could play on our imaginations, but a presence which seemingly twice leaves us as an investigator does? A woman being pushed against the wall? Another man hearing a slapping sound in roughly the same place and two separate witnesses claiming to see a dark robed figure following me around as I traversed the galleries? All imagination? Who knows – I'll have to find out more on my next visit to the Castle Keep.

Visitor Information

Address:
Castle Keep
Castle Garth
Newcastle-upon-Tyne
NE1 1RQ

Tel: 0191 2327938
Website: museums.ncl.ac.uk/keep

Opening Hours: April–September, daily 9.30 a.m.–5.30 p.m.; October–March, daily 9.30 a.m.–4.30 p.m.
Closed Good Friday, Christmas Day, Boxing Day, New Years Day
Last entry 30 minutes before closing time
The Black Gate is accessible at all times

How to Get There: The Castle Keep can be found close to the Bigg Market, opposite the Bridge Hotel public house, next to the High Level Bridge

Additional Information:
- There are virtual tours of the Castle Keep and the Black Gate on the Castle's website
- The Castle Keep is not suitable for wheelchair users
- There is a small visitor shop within the keep
- There are no toilet facilities
- The keep holds Theatre and Entertainment licences and is used for a wide variety of functions and events, the keep often hosts wedding receptions and other celebrations
- There are a large number of organised paranormal investigations carried out at the keep, many of which are open to the public at a cost. However, these are not organised by the castle, they are organised by the many paranormal teams in the region

The Cathedral Church of St Nicholas

*T*he Cathedral Church of St Nicholas in Newcastle-upon-Tyne began life as a parish church named for the patron saint of sailors. The church was built in 1091, shortly after work has been completed, in 1080, on Newcastle's Castle Garth. The wooden church was rebuilt in stone in the twelfth century and suffered damage from fire in 1216, being restored in 1359. The church was improved and expanded over the years that followed and at the end of the fifteenth century the lantern tower was built, standing almost 200ft high.

During a siege by the Scottish in 1644 the church was surrounded and the Scottish general threatened to destroy St Nicholas' Church unless the keys to the walled city

The cathedral's graveyard. (By kind permission of The Cathedral Church of St Nicholas)

The Cathedral Church of St Nicholas. (By kind permission of
The Cathedral Church of St Nicholas)

The effigy of the unknown knight believed to haunt the cathedral. (By kind permission of The Cathedral Church of St Nicholas)

were handed over to them. The mayor of Newcastle had over 100 Scottish prisoners brought to the church and placed in the tower. The Scots relented, realising that opening cannon fire on the church would result in the death of their own. A number of the Scottish prisoners had been very ill prior to this and were in a great deal of pain while being moved. Several of them died whilst being held in the church.

St Nicholas' Church became a cathedral in 1882 when the Diocese of Newcastle was created by Queen Victoria.

I spoke with Steve Taylor of aloneinthedarkentertainment.com and founder of the Newcastle's Ghost Walk, and he told me of the restless spirit of a woman called Martha Williams who was murdered in the graveyard at St Nicholas' Cathedral:

A medium told us of a grave robbery that went wrong. Two grave robbers were digging up corpses late at night when two ladies took a short cut through the graveyard. The ladies got into an argument and one of them, a woman named Rebecca Wood, stormed off. Rebecca walked past the grave robbers, who were aware of the women and had realised they may have potentially found themselves two fresher corpses. As Rebecca was leaving the graveyard she heard a scream, one of the grave robbers had snuck up behind her friend Martha Williams and struck her across the head with his shovel. As Martha hit the ground, Rebecca started to scream, she too was knocked unconscious and both women were sexually assaulted by the grave robbers. The police had been alerted by the screaming and headed to the graveyard, but were too late. As the police arrived, blowing their whistles and shouting for whoever was there to give themselves up, the grave robbers fled the scene with Rebecca Wood. The battered and raped body of Martha Williams was found by the police slumped next to a grave, she had been hit repeatedly across the head by a shovel until dead. The fate of Rebecca Wood is unknown.

To this day, people still see the spectral form of Martha Williams in the graveyard standing in the area where her body was found. Those who have seen her have said that she holds one hand to her face and from behind it could be mistaken for someone talking on a mobile phone. Mediums have said that she does this to try and hide the scars from the shovel blade.

Even local police have seen Martha at night standing alone facing the cathedral and when they have called out to ask if she needs any help, she never replies. When they approach her she simply disappears.

There have been reports of a moaning heard inside the cathedral, the sound reverberating throughout the cathedral, making it impossible to locate the source of the disembodied cries of someone seemingly in pain. This sound has been attributed to the restless spirits of the Scottish prisoners who died in the building over 350 years ago during the siege on the city of Newcastle.

A ghostly knight has also been seen in the cathedral, by both day and night. He vanishes as he passes pillars. The clanking sound of armour has also been heard. The identity of this phantom knight is unknown, although it is believed that it may be the spirit of the 'unknown knight' of which there is an effigy within the cathedral. The effigy was thrown out of the cathedral in 1783, but was later returned by the parish clerk.

Visitor Information

Address:
The Cathedral Church of St Nicholas
St Nicholas' Churchyard
Newcastle-upon-Tyne
NE1 1PF

Tel: 0191 2321939
Website: www.newcastle-ang-cathedral-stnicholas.org.uk
Email: office@stnicnewcastle.co.uk

How to Get There: The cathedral is found in Newcastle city centre on the corner of St Nicholas Street and Mosley Street

Additional Information:
- The cathedral shop is open Monday–Friday 10 a.m.–2.30 p.m., and stocks a wide range of ornaments, greetings cards, postcards, prayer cards, souvenirs, tapes and CDs, including all the cathedral choir's recent recordings
- The cathedral refectory is open Monday–Friday 10 a.m.–2.30 p.m.
- The cathedral offers meeting and conferencing rooms, please contact the cathedral or visit their website for further details
- Newcastle's Ghost Walk runs every Friday, Saturday and Sunday, at 7 p.m. and 8.30 p.m. There is no need to pre-book, simply turn up on the night at the meeting point outside the Castle Keep fifteen minutes before the walk is due to begin. Tickets can be pre-booked if desired at Isis Mind, Body & Spirit, Newcastle Tourist Information Centre, the Castle Keep, or at www.aloneinthedarkentertainment.com. For further information please call 0191 4403196 or visit the website. Information can also be found on the site about organised paranormal investigations

The Central Arcade

*T*he Central Arcade was originally built in 1838 by Richard Grainger. An elegant design, it was intended for use as a corn market, but it was badly received by the town's authorities, and instead was used as a news room until 1867 when the arcade was ravaged by fire. It was rebuilt and reopened as an art gallery and concert hall. Again, the building generated little interest, and due to lack of visitors it closed down only two years later in 1869.

In 1870, the building was leased by a partnership, T.P. Barkas and T.H. Twedy, and they reopened the Central Arcade as an art gallery and news room. The venture was a great success and improvements were made. By 1892, the Central Exchange News Room, as it was now named, contained an art gallery and a magnificent concert hall capable of seating over 1,000 people. The Central Exchange Hotel was also opened, overlooking Grey Street and Market Street. The hotel was run by John Dykes and contained a billiard room, smoking rooms, sitting rooms, and fifty bedrooms. A local legend is that a young woman working at the hotel discovered she was pregnant. Terrified of losing her job and the support of her family, she threw herself down the hotel lift shaft to her inevitable end, and the death of her unborn child.

Fire struck again in 1901 and the building was destroyed. Rebuilding took place and the Central Arcade was reopened in 1906 as an impressive shopping centre featuring an impressive mosaic tiled floor. Visitors to the Central Arcade today will discover that the magnificent building's decoration remains as it appeared when it was reopened over 100 years ago.

Many locals refer to the Central Arcade as 'Windows Arcade' on account of the music shop, JG Windows that takes up much of the shop space. JG Windows is one of the oldest music shops in the UK, celebrating its centenary in 2008. The shop stands on the site of the old Central Exchange Hotel. Customers and staff have reported inexplicable happenings, in particular in the basement, home to the instrument department, which happens to be the location where the base of the old hotel lift shaft once was. Staff have reported being tapped on the shoulder, and pushed in the back when in a room completely alone. Disembodied moaning has been heard on a number of occasions, and CDs have flown off shelves without anyone being near them.

The Central Arcade.

One day when the shop was closed a member of staff was coming up the stairs from the basement and was nearing the top when they could clearly hear the sound of someone running up the stairs behind them. This member of staff was the only person in the shop at the time. Terrified, they turned around expecting to see someone, or something, appear behind them. The footsteps got closer, until they sounded like they were running past, or maybe even through them! The footsteps seemed to reach the top of the steps and then stopped.

Elsewhere in the Central Arcade a young lady wearing servant's clothes has been seen, always repeating the same short journey through the same part of the Arcade before walking through a wall.

During the 1980s there were a number of reports of a spectral man seen stumbling through the Arcade bleeding from the head, mouth, and eyes. He walks with his arms outstretched as if in pain and seeking help, heading towards the Grey Street exit before vanishing.

Visitor Information

Address:
Central Arcade
Newcastle-upon-Tyne
NE1 5BP

Tel: 0191 2321356 (JG Windows)
Website: www.jgwindows.com (JG Windows)
Email: info@jgwindows.com (JG Windows)

Opening Hours: Monday, Tuesday, Wednesday, Friday and Saturday 9 a.m.–5.30 p.m., Thursday 9 a.m.–7 p.m. (JG Windows)

How to Get There: Central Arcade is in Newcastle city centre and has three entrances – Grey Street and Grainger Street (both next to Grey's Monument), and also in Market Street

Additional Information:
- Newcastle's Tourist Information Centre is located within the Central Arcade
- Please note there are no toilet facilities within the Central Arcade

The Cooperage

The Cooperage on Newcastle's quayside is one of the oldest surviving buildings in the city, dating back to the fourteenth century. The exterior of the building has changed little throughout the Cooperage's history, and the large beams in the main bar are over 600 years old. Over the centuries the building has been used as a warehouse, a merchant's house, and in 1853 John Arthur took over the building and used it as a cooperage, where barrels were manufactured and sold to the public houses throughout the city.

In 1973, the Cooperage opened as a bar and restaurant, and immediately staff and customers began to experience paranormal happenings. Reports continue to this day, resulting in the Cooperage being considered one of the most haunted locations in Newcastle-upon-Tyne.

One of the most commonly experienced phenomena is the sound of footsteps coming down the staircase when the pub is closed and the only people present are staff, none of whom are in that area. Disembodied shouting has also been heard on a number of occasions.

Full spectral apparitions of four different spirits have been witnessed throughout the building; a former cleaner witnessed a young girl in a shimmering dress, combing her long blonde hair; a number of people have seen a man wearing a top hat watching out of a second floor window; the transparent figure of a woman has been seen in the restaurant area, described by one witness as almost looking like a grainy washed-out photograph from the past; and a former member of staff saw a ghostly man appear, then change colour before vanishing before his eyes.

The best known ghost in the area is not in the Cooperage itself, it is the haunting figure who is seen on the steep stairway named 'the Long Stairs' running alongside the Cooperage. During the sixteenth century, press gangs were a common sight on Newcastle's quayside, rounding up able-bodied men to work on board their ships against their will, leaving their loved ones unaware of the reason for their men's disappearance. A man by the name of Henry Hardwick was walking along the quayside and was grabbed by a press gang along with a number of other reluctant men. Terrified by the prospect of being forced to go to sea, Hardwick rallied the small band of locals to fight back. They punched and kicked their way to freedom and made a run for it. Hardwick's freedom was unfortunately short-lived; he was

The Cooperage.

chased to the top of the steep staircase by the side of the Cooperage and caught by the press gang. For his reluctance to go willingly they plucked out his eyeballs before throwing him down the staircase and ending his life. To this day there are reports by terrified witnesses of a man seen staggering down the stairs with blood running down his face and voids where his eyes once were.

Steve Taylor of Alone in the Dark Entertainment told me of what he encountered on an overnight vigil at the Cooperage, organised by Ghost Hunters Team UK:

The Cooperage is a truly amazing place to carry out a ghost hunt, although the place can be quite noisy with creaking floorboards and the natural groans of the old building. On the night we spent there the Cooperage did not disappoint, the most amazing thing was witnessed through a night vision camera, but for some inexplicable reason what we saw did not record even though it appeared to be working fine at the time. We had split up into two teams. I was with team one and we were watching team two conduct a séance through a monitor in another room. We were all shocked when one of our team noticed an extra person sitting in one of the spare seats at the table with the second team. We could all see it, a small girl appeared to be sat at the table with them. We contacted them via two-way radio and told them we could

The Long Stairs; the scene of the brutal murder of Henry Hardwick.

see an extra person at the table, but gave them no indication as to what that person looked like. They responded and said there was no one else with them, although the air temperature in the room had just dropped from 16°c down to just 9°c. Suddenly the glass started moving and team two continued to ask questions, the spirit they had contacted was the spirit of a young girl. All this time we could still see the girl, she would shuffle in her seat, then vanish, then reappear and play with her hair. It was chilling.

Visitor Information

Address:
The Cooperage
32 The Close
Newcastle-upon-Tyne
NE1 3RF

Tel: 0191 2 332940
Website: www.cooperage1730.co.uk

Opening Hours: Monday 5 p.m.–2.30 a.m., Tuesday, Wednesday and Thursday 5 p.m.–1.30 a.m., Friday and Saturday 2 p.m.–3 a.m.
Occasionally closing times may vary depending on promotions and live music

How to Get There: The Cooperage is situated on the quayside near to the Swing Bridge

Additional Information:
- A cash machine is available inside the Cooperage
- A function room is available for hire with party bookings taken
- Food is served daily from 9 a.m.–3 p.m. Eat in or takeaway
- 'Alone in the Dark Entertainment' organise regular paranormal investigations at the Cooperage. Please visit www.aloneinthedarkentertainment.com for further information

Gibside

George Bowes, born in 1701, was the eldest son of the MP Sir William Bowes and Elizabeth Bowes. In 1713, George's father took ownership of the Gibside estate which included some of the north's richest coal seams and led to the Bowes family becoming incredibly wealthy.

George Bowes inherited the family estates in 1721 and with his newly acquired wealth he began work on a magnificent forest garden set in fifteen miles of woodland at Gibside. Bowes designed the follies and the walks himself, including the Great Walk which is over half a mile in length. The house was improved and a large kitchen block added. A stable block was added in 1746, and a banqueting house in 1752. In 1757 the Column of British Liberty was built at the north end of the Great Walk, a statue by Christopher Richardson standing 140ft high.

In October 1724 he married fourteen-year-old Eleanor Verney, but she died three months later. It was believed by many at the time that her death was as a result of her husband's insatiable sexual appetite.

Bowes was a widower for nineteen years before he married Mary Gilbert in 1747 and they had one daughter, Mary Eleanor Bowes, the following year. She married John Lyon, 9th Earl of Strathmore and Kinghorne, who later took the name 'Bowes', as a condition of the will of George Bowes, in order to inherit the Bowes estate. They formed the Bowes-Lyon family, one of whose descendants was the late Elizabeth Bowes-Lyon, better known as the Queen Mother.

Bowes was for some years the MP for County Durham and he was very influential, largely on account of the coal which lay beneath his estates. In 1726 the Grand Alliance of coal owners was founded, Bowes being a founder member.

In 1760, shortly after work was begun on the orangery and chapel, designed to be a family mausoleum, George Bowes died at Gibside. His estates passed to his son-in-law. Bowes was buried at Whickham, County Durham. Work on the chapel was left unfinished for many years, until it was finally completed in 1812, at which time George Bowes body was moved into the mausoleum.

Countess Mary Eleanor Bowes and the earl had five children between 1768 and 1773, but despite this the marriage was an unhappy one. In 1773 the earl died of consumption. The countess did not grieve for her husband and began a relationship with a man called George Grey. She fell pregnant to him, and while pregnant with

Gibside in autumn. The chapel stands at the end of the Great Walk.
(By kind permission of the National Trust)

Grey's child she married another man, Andrew Robinson Shorey. Shorey changed his name to Bowes in line with George Bowes' will.

Andrew was a cruel and unkind husband, he knew he had married into a weathy family and sought money from his wife constantly. He would beat her and starve her. It was not uncommon for her to be locked inside a cupboard within Gibside Hall. He sold her London house, and felled many trees within the woodland at Gibside to sell to fund his extravagant lifestyle. She eventually managed to get a divorce in 1789, and died in 1800 after living a quiet life in Hampshire. It had always been her wish to be laid to rest in the family mausoleum at Gibside, but she was buried at Westminister Abbey.

Gibside stayed in the Bowes family until 1885 when the family line ended with John Bowes, George Bowes great-grandson, who died childless.

The orangery. (By kind permission of the National Trust)

Gibside Hall was never lived in again and the estate fell into decline. During the 1940s many trees were felled to help the war effort. In 1965, the National Trust stepped in and restoration work began on the decaying chapel, followed by plans to restore the character of the woodland. Gibside is home to a wide species of birds and animals, such as the red kite which was on the brink of extinction in the British Isles less than thirty years ago.

A ghostly form has been seen gliding across the grounds towards the orangery, it is believed that this is the spirit of Mary Eleanor Bowes who loved Gibside so much but was not laid to rest there, despite her wishes. A piano has been heard playing within the ruin of Gibside Hall, and visitors have also experienced the strong smell of perfume in the chapel.

Visitor Information

Address:
Gibside
Nr Rowlands Gill
Burnopfield
Tyne and Wear
NE16 6BG

Tel: 01207 541820
Website: www.nationaltrust.org.uk/main/w-gibside
Email: gibside@nationaltrust.org.uk

Opening Hours: The grounds at Gibside are open all year round with the exception of the Christmas and New Year period. The chapel is open March–November. The opening times vary annually, further information can be found on the website or by calling the National Trust

How to Get There: Gibside is signposted from the A1; heading northbound it is the exit after the Metro Centre, heading southbound it is the exit before the Metro Centre

Additional Information:
- Gift shop with regional products
- Dogs are allowed in the grounds, but should be kept on a lead
- Tea room serves light lunches, there is also a kiosk serving ice cream and refreshments
- Baby changing facilities are available, and push chairs and baby back-carriers are admitted
- Suitable for school groups. Please contact National Trust for further information
- Guided tour and refreshments are available by arrangement
- Weddings can be performed at Gibside. Please visit the website for further details

Hylton Castle

*T*he first castle on the site that Hylton Castle occupies to this day is likely to have been built in wood. It was built by Henry de Hilton in 1072 close to the south bank of the River Tyne on land granted to him by William I. Between 1374 and 1420, the castle and St Catherine's Chapel in the castle grounds were rebuilt in stone by Sir William Hilton. The castle was redesigned as a four-storey, fortified manor house.

The castle stayed in the Hilton family until 1640, when Baron Henry Hilton died and left the castle to the Corporation of London with the agreement that the castle would be used for charitable purposes for the following ninety-nine years. A legal battle ensued and a number of years later the castle was returned to the family at great expense, and Baron Henry's nephew, John, became the legal owner of the castle. In the years that followed the castle was improved significantly, most notably in the early 1700s when the interior was completely redesigned on three levels, and a three-storey north wing was added. Improvements were made to the chapel, and a complimentary south wing added later by the last Baron Hilton, prior to his death in 1746. With no male heir, the castle was passed into the hands of his nephew, Sir Richard Musgrave. Sir Richard changed his name to Hylton, and with this the spelling of the castle's name would be changed forever. Sir Richard Hylton sold the castle in 1755 to Lady Mary Bowes, widow of Sir George Bowes. However, she never lived in the castle.

The castle fell into a state of decay, until 1812 when a local businessman, Simon Temple, leased the castle and work began to make it habitable once again. The castle was restored, the chapel was re-roofed, and the gardens were cultivated. Unfortunately Temple's business ventures were failing so his work had ceased by 1819.

Hylton Castle changed hands several times, and between 1840 and 1842 it was even used as a boarding school. In January of 1856, the castle burnt down while in the ownership of one Mr McLaren, a farmer.

In 1862 the castle was bought by William Briggs, a local timber merchant. Briggs intended to return the castle to how he envisaged it would have appeared in its medieval heyday. He demolished the north and south wings and gutted the interior of the castle. A number of cosmetic changed were made, including the windows

Hylton Castle. (By kind permission of English Heritage)

being amended, as was the gothic doorway. Upon Brigg's death in 1871, the castle passed into the hands of his son, Colonel Charles James Briggs.

By 1930 the castle had fallen into ruin, and the lead from the castle roof had been stolen. In 1950 the Ministry of Works stepped in and took over ownership of the castle. The missing lead on the roof was covered over with roofing felt to ensure that the castle was waterproof, and all internal partitions were removed.

These days the ruin of Hylton Castle is best known for its resident ghost, the Cauld Lad. At the beginning of the seventeenth century Sir Robert Hilton, the 13th Baron Hilton, was the owner of the castle, and on one fateful day he waited impatiently for his horse to be saddled in readiness for a fox hunt. He found the stable-boy, young Roger Skelton, asleep in the hay and in a fit of rage he took a pitchfork and bayoneted Roger. The young boy died almost instantly. The baron's anger gave way to panic as he realised the gravity of his actions. He covered Roger's lifeless body in hay, saddled his own horse and rode into the castle courtyard. He was keen to tell anyone who would listen that he had caught the stable-boy sleeping so had ordered him to leave the castle and never return.

St Catherine's Chapel. (By kind permission of English Heritage)

That night the baron went to the stable under the cover of darkness, wrapped Roger's corpse in a blanket and threw the body in a deep pond nearby. The baron had been careful to leave no evidence, but not careful enough it seems, for it is historical fact that he was tried in July 1609 for the murder of Roger Skelton. Sir Robert Hilton was found guilty, but, due to the lack of a body, was later given a full pardon. It seems that the ghost of young Roger Skelton could not rest in peace in the knowledge that his killer would not pay for his crime; from that day forth Hylton Castle was plagued with paranormal occurrences.

Late at night wails and cries could be heard throughout the castle, and on numerous occasions, terrified servants living in the castle would see the ghost of Skelton, always naked, crying out 'I'm cauld, I'm cauld' before disappearing, earning the ghost the nickname of the Cauld Lad. The ghost could be quite helpful, if a mess was left in the kitchen, the servants would find the kitchen spotless the following morning. However, if there were no tasks left for the Cauld Lad to do at night, then he would cause mayhem, mixing up salt and sugar, emptying chamber pots onto the floor, and breaking crockery.

The interior of Hylton Castle, taken during a special open day in September 2008.
(By kind permission of English Heritage)

The disturbances continued for almost 100 years until 1703, when a pond close to the castle was drained and the skeleton of a male aged eleven or twelve was recovered. It is believed that these were the remains of Roger Skelton. The body was given a Christian burial and the nightly phenomena at the castle seemed to cease.

Over three centuries have passed since the Cauld Lad found peace and is said to have left the castle, but to this day strange happenings are still being reported at Hylton Castle. A local newspaper ran a story in 1970 of a miner coming home from a nearby pit. He heard a voice call out to him from the castle grounds, and as he turned to look a dark figure materialised alongside him. The miner was understandably terrified and ran as fast as he could towards home, almost too scared to turn his head for fear that something may still be there. As he saw the safety of his house he plucked up the courage to turn his head to the side. His blood ran cold as he saw the dark figure running alongside him. He got home and slammed the door shut behind him. He pulled back the curtain and looked outside and the dark being remained there completely motionless for the next few hours before simply disappearing.

In the late 1970s there was a spate of reports of large lights seen moving around the top of Hylton Castle at night, although the upper floors of the castle had been removed.

In the 1980s local residents were woken in the middle of the night by a high-pitched screaming. It was so loud and distressing that many people left their homes to come outside and see what the commotion was. The noise was coming from Hylton Castle. The screaming continued for almost an hour and the police were called for fear that a woman, or child, were being attacked, sexually assaulted, or even murdered. Police officers searched the castle, the chapel, and the grounds, as the blood-curdling screaming continued, unable to pinpoint precisely where the noise was coming from. The screaming stopped as suddenly as it had begun; the source of the disturbing sound was never explained.

The castle was declared unsafe for visitors several years ago and the inside of the castle is currently inaccessible. Despite this, a number of people have reported hearing loud bangs and laughter coming from inside the castle itself, often late at night.

St Catherine's Chapel, where a number of the Hilton family were buried, has also been the scene of some unusual goings-on, visitors have reported having stones thrown at them, even though they have often been the only person there. There have also been sightings of a spectral nun walking through the chapel.

Visitor Information

Address:
Hylton Castle
Craigavon Road
Hylton Castle Estate
Sunderland
SR5 3PA

Website: www.english-heritage.org.uk

Opening Hours: Any reasonable time (grounds and St Catherine's Chapel only)

How to Get There: The castle is signposted from the A1231, three-and-three-quarter miles west of Sunderland

Additional Information:
- There is a car park and the grounds are suitable for disabled visitors
- The inside of the castle is currently considered unsafe and is inaccessible to visitors. However, in 1999 the Friends of Hylton Dene was formed by residents of the estates around Hylton Dene with the aim of co-operating with Sunderland City Council, Durham Wildlife Trust and other agencies to actively involve the local community in the development and upkeep of Hylton Dene and castle. The Friends of Hylton Dene are currently working alongside English Heritage and Sunderland City Council to assess the feasibility of renovating the interior of the castle to make it safe to open to the public once again, work will hopefully begin in 2010. For further information, and updates, please go to www.hyltoncastle.com
- There are occasional open days where access to the interior of the castle is permitted. Please go to www.hyltoncastle.com for news of forthcoming events

The Journal Tyne Theatre

*T*he Journal Tyne Theatre is one of the region's most popular live-entertainment venues and is the oldest working Victorian theatre in the world. It was opened on 18 September 1867 as the Tyne Theatre and Opera House. The theatre was designed by William B. Parnell, and has changed hands, and been renamed, many times over the years. The current operators of the theatre are SMG, who own the Metro Radio Arena, backed by the *Journal* newspaper, and was renamed in recent years as the Journal Tyne Theatre.

It remains today much as it was when it first opened, including the frontage which remains almost identical to how it would have appeared in 1867.

On 7 April 1887, a terrible accident took place at the Tyne Theatre and Opera House. The theatre had a revolutionary sound effect system, and during the performance of an opera *Nordisa* a cannon ball, weighing 36lbs, was rolled along a surface to generate a thunder sound on stage. The ball then dropped into a box and the sound effect ceased. However, on that fateful night the ball fell out of the box, falling a distance of 12ft and landed on the head of a member of staff, Bob Courtenedge, shattering his skull and killing him instantly.

The ghost of Bob is believed to have haunted the Tyne Theatre ever since that tragic night over 130 years ago, with literally hundreds of people claiming to have seen him. The smell of tobacco has also been reported by staff in the theatre, especially after a performance has finished, and the theatre-goers have dispersed into the night.

The Journal Tyne Theatre. (Photograph provided courtesy of the Journal Tyne Theatre)

The auditorium. (Photograph provided courtesy of the Journal Tyne Theatre)

Visitor Information

Address:
The Journal Tyne Theatre
Westgate Road
Newcastle-upon-Tyne
NE1 4AG

Tel: 0844 4934567
Website: www.thejournaltynetheatre.co.uk

Opening Hours: Opening times vary depending on events taking place. Please visit the website or call the Journal Tyne Theatre for further information

How to Get There: The Journal Tyne Theatre is close to the A1, take the A184 signposted City Centre and follow that road, which becomes the A189, and leads into St James Boulevard. This will bring you to a right turn (Nexus Building) onto Westgate Road A186, where the Theatre is situated on the right-hand side

Additional Information:
- The theatre is available for hire for corporate events, seminars and conferences
- The theatre is suitable for wheelchairs
- There is an events newsletter – which can be signed up to on the website – for regular news on forthcoming events

Marsden Grotto

In 1782 Jack Bates, an unemployed miner from Allendale, moved to Marsden in South Shields looking for work. Without the money to buy a house, he discovered the many caves hidden within Marsden Bay's limestone cliff face, and set about expanding one of them with explosives until it was a good size for himself and his wife to live in comfortably. This earned Jack the nickname of 'the Blaster'. Jack found it hard to come by work and it is believed that in order to earn money he may have had illicit dealings with the many smugglers who came ashore at Marsden Bay, and had used the caves for centuries to hide their contraband. In 1788 Jack carved out stone steps from the beach to the cliff top. The stairs that are there nowadays still carry the nickname 'Jack the Blaster's stairs'. In 1792, Jack the Blaster died and his widow moved away from the area leaving their unusual home empty.

Peter Allan decided to move into the cave in 1826, expanding it further and making it more accessible. During the excavations eighteen human skeletons were uncovered, believed to be the remains of smugglers who met their end due to their unlawful dealings, and in most instances likely to have been double-crossed by their own kind.

The improvements took a number of years but Allan successfully constructed a two-storey cave, complete with a basic kitchen, and it was opened as an inn named the Tam O'Shanter, renamed shortly after as the Marsden Grotto. The inn proved popular with the smugglers of the day and the landlord turned a blind eye to their illegal activities, often hiding cargo for them, in return for their valued custom.

In 1849, Peter Allan passed away and his wife and children continued to run the inn. There were several freak high tides which hit Marsden Bay during the 1850s, resulting in the death of several smugglers on the beach and in the caves, and also flooding the Marsden Grotto resulting in costly repairs on each occasion. In 1865 a cliff face collapsed, damaging the inn considerably. In 1874 the Allan family left the Marsden Grotto.

The business was taken over by Sidney Milnes Hawkes and improvements were made to the interior and to make the building structurally sound. Marsden Grotto was then sold on to the Vaux brewery in 1898; they installed the lift and ran the business successfully for over a century, before selling it on in 1999. Today the Marsden Grotto is still a very popular restaurant and bar.

Marsden Grotto. (By kind permission of Marsden Grotto)

The Marsden Grotto, the only 'cave-bar' in Europe, is an amazing place; there are rumours of hidden rooms within the Grotto waiting to be discovered. It is also widely regarded as the most haunted public house in England. Banging, whispering, and screaming have been heard. Sightings of fully formed apparitions are commonly reported, attributed to the building being steeped in violence, double-crossing, and cruelty.

In the 1840s a smuggler willingly sold information to a HM customs officer, other smugglers got word of this and confronted him one rainy night on the beach outside the Marsden Grotto. The smuggler was only too aware that if they knew the truth they'd kill him. He made a run for it but was quickly caught. He begged for his life but his captors showed no mercy, raining blows down on him and breaking his arms and legs in multiple places. They then put him into a barrel used for transporting their illegal goods, barely large enough for him to fit inside. They nailed the lid down as he became hysterical, pleading with them to stop. They placed the barrel deep inside one of the caves in the cliff face where he was left to die. His screams of desperation and hunger were heard for several days until he died. It is believed the barrel was never recovered and the dead smuggler's skeletal remains are still inside that barrel to this day, hidden in one of the many caves at

The Cave Bar. (By kind permission of Marsden Grotto)

Marsden Bay. On stormy nights as the rain lashes down and the wild wind blows, his ghost can still be heard screaming out in terror.

Several years later an HM customs officer went to the Marsden Grotto and befriended a smuggler who was a regular customer; the smuggler was unaware of his new friend's occupation. The officer showed a keen interest in how the smuggler earned his money, and asked a lot of questions, the smuggler trusted him and told all. He eventually realised what was going on and a fight broke out between the pair, the smuggler was shot and died in the inn. Peter Allan emptied the smuggler's tankard and nailed it to the wall, proclaiming that if anyone should drink from the tankard they would be cursed, and if the tankard was removed from Marsden Grotto the ghost of the dead smuggler would return and haunt the building forever more.

The tankard on display is not the original, it's a replica. The original vanished many years ago. Many belive that the ghost of the murdered smuggler still remains at the Grotto to this day and that it is responsible for much of the inexplicable phenomena reported on almost a daily basis.

I spoke to Suzanne Hitchinson about an investigation at Marsden Grotto in 2005 that she was asked to partake in:

Marsden Bay; home to the Shoney.

The most notable thing to happen was in the Cave Bar, we were sitting quietly waiting for any spirits to make themselves known when I saw what appeared to be a black silhouette standing next to the pool table. I was with another investigator and he also confirmed he could see this black mass. We sat and watched it for about forty seconds before it disappeared.

The Marsden Grotto undoubtedly has a truly fascinating, bloody past to match any building in the region. However, Marsden Bay itself could claim to have an even more impressive history, and in particular the legend of its very own sea monster; the Shoney.

Belief that a sea monster lurks beneath the North Sea at Marsden dates back to ninth century, when the north east of England was under the control of the Vikings.

The Shoney is a Viking name, and the Norsemen took the threat of the monster very seriously. In order to pass Marsden Bay safely they would offer a human sacrifice to the Shoney. The crewmembers would draw lots and the loser would have his hands and feet trussed and his throat slit, then be thrown overboard. The Vikings believed the Shoney would take the sacrifice to his underwater lair and allow the Viking longships to pass. This tradition was carried on by Scandinavian sailors until well into the twelfth century. Bodies were washed up all along the coastline, as far north as Lindisfarne, sometimes they were untouched, but occasionally appeared to be half eaten. The last body washed up at Marsden Bay was in 1928.

Despite the Shoney appearing to be a mythical beast feared by superstitious Vikings almost 1,200 years ago, there have been a large number of reported sightings of an unusual sea creature at Marsden Bay over the years. Mike Hallowell, author of several books including the *Mystery Animals of the British Isles: Northumberland and Tyneside*, and co-author of *The South Shields Poltergeist: One Family's Fight Against an Invisible Intruder*, told me of his potential sighting of the Shoney in August 1998:

> I was driving along the coast towards Whitburn with my father and my wife when I looked towards the sea at Marsden Bay. About thirty yards from the shore was a huge, brown 'thing' breaking the surface of the water. Although only a small 'hump' appeared to be above water level, I could see a much larger area just beneath the surface. I thought that I must have been seeing things so I shouted to my wife to look to see if she could see it too.
>
> My wife could also see it, although neither of us knew what it could be. We parked at the next opportunity and looked out to sea again. It was still there, it had completely vanished beneath the water, but through the waves we could still see its brown colour, although the shape was indistinct. After what seemed like no more than a couple of minutes we lost sight of it.
>
> When we arrived home, we saw the front page of that evening's *Shields' Gazette* which was of a dolphin that had been seen at Marsden Bay and had been nicknamed Daphne the Dolphin. We both thought that it may well have seen Daphne for ourselves, however the creature we saw was far too big to be a dolphin, and was also the wrong colour.
>
> I then received a phone call from a local councillor on an unrelated matter, and I happened to mention Daphne the Dolphin and that I thought I may have seen her, although I explained that what I saw seemed much larger than a bottlenose dolphin.
>
> 'Funny you should mention that,' said the councillor, 'I was buying some fish and chips in South Shields when I overheard two men in the queue talking about something they had seen at Marsden Bay. I overheard one of them say, "No way was that a dolphin. What I saw could have swallowed a dolphin in one gulp."'

Visitor Information

Address:
The Marsden Grotto
Coast Road
South Shields
Tyne and Wear
NE34 7BS

Tel: 0191 4556060
Website: www.marsden-grotto.co.uk

Opening Hours:
Monday–Thursday 8 a.m.–9 p.m., Friday and Saturday 8 a.m.–midnight, Sunday 10 a.m.–midnight

How to Get There: The Grotto is found on the A183 (Coast Road) in South Shields, close to Souter Lighthouse and South Shields Golf Club

Additional Information:
- Breakfast is served Monday–Saturday 8 a.m.–midday. A full menu is available from midday–8 p.m. on Monday–Saturday, and midday–6 p.m. on Sunday
- The Marsden Grotto comprises of the restaurant, the Oyster Bar, and the Cave Bar
- Marsden Grotto has a beach shop offering everything from buckets and spades to suntan lotion, and has a number or organised beach activities. Please contact Marsden Grotto for further information

The North East Aircraft Museum

In the autumn of 1916 RAF Usworth opened on West Town Moor on a stretch of land north of the River Wear between Washington and Sunderland. The airfield was used by 36 Squadron, the region's Home Defence unit. By the summer of 1917 the Squadron HQ was based at the airfield, with the Bristol Fighter being the primary aircraft in use. In June 1919, 36 Squadron was disbanded and the grass airfield no longer served a purpose.

In March 1930, the 607 Squadron of the Royal Auxiliary Air Force moved onto the unused airfield. During the war, the airfield was improved to include a perimeter track and two runways. Squadron 607, equipped with Hurricane aircraft between June 1940 and early 1941, were actively involved with the war effort. On 15 August 1940 every single aircraft from RAF Usworth was in action, shooting down a great many German Heinkel and Messerschmitt 110 fighters over the north-eastern coastline.

On 3 July 1962, the airfield became Sunderland Airport after being purchased by Sunderland Corporation. In 1974 a group of like-minded vintage aircraft enthusiasts began meeting at the airport regularly, forming a club and establishing a site in Lambton were they began to form a collection of aircraft, which, after several name changes, would go on to become the North East Aircraft Museum. In 1977 the museum was moved to Sunderland Airport.

In 1984, Sunderland Airport was closed to make way for a Nissan car factory, and the North East Aircraft Museum was moved to a four acre site just outside the boundary of the airport, where it remains to this day.

The North East Aircraft Museum has gained a reputation in recent years as one of the most active haunted locations in the region, with dark shadows and poltergeist activity experienced regularly in all three hangars on the site.

One of the most regular occurrences involves an air-sea rescue helicopter which was involved in the rescue of Falkland war troops from the ship *Sir Galahad* in June 1982. The spirit of a pilot is very protective of 'his' helicopter and has been seen on a number of occasions. More commonly people have been pushed by unseen hands when standing close to the helicopter.

The haunted hangars at the North East Aircraft Museum.
(By kind permission of the North East Aircraft Museum)

Another spirit linked to the museum is that of Edward Grenville Shaw. Shaw was a pilot in training during the Second World War, and on 12 March 1942 he was involved in a routine training exercise involving two trainee pilots flying Hurricanes towards each other. Unfortunately they clipped wings and Shaw's plane crashed a short distance away. He had been thrown from his plane in the impact and was killed instantly. His body was found in boggy ground and when recovered his boots were left behind.

The ghost of a man, believed to be Shaw, has been seen on a number of occasions calling out for help in the Display Hall in Hangar Three. The same man has been seen wandering in the Display Hall, where the wreckage of his crashed Hurricane is on display.

The ghost of a German spy who stole a plane to escape during the Second World War, and was later hanged in Germany for a separate crime is often seen throughout the museum.

Other occurrences are stones being thrown in Hangar One, the ghost of an Alsatian dog seen and heard across the site, and the noise of wartime music and chatter has been heard. A former Navy aircraft in Hangar Two has been seen to shudder and shake inexplicably.

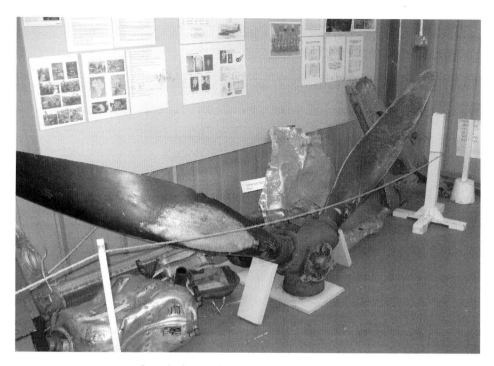

Parts of wrecked aircraft are on display in the Display Hall.
(By kind permission of the North East Aircraft Museum)

A spirit, known as George by the staff, has been seen countless times. It is believed that during the war he was asleep on the roof of one of the hangars on the old airfield during a hot summer day. He woke with a start and rolled off the roof to his death.

North East Supernatural Research spent a night investigating the North East Aircraft Museum in May 2007. Ethel Turnbull, one of the core team members, told me of their findings:

North East Supernatural Research decided to investigate the North East Aircraft Museum after hearing so many stories about what people had been experiencing there. During the evening we saw several dark shapes following us around all three of the hangers. We also saw someone in a blue outfit similar to a boiler suit walk behind one of the hangars.

A few small stones, or what we presume were stones as the noise was quite loud, were thrown at us in one of the smaller hangars. Darrin, the other Core Team Investigator had a two pence piece thrown at him, which he found lying next to him on the floor. The shuffling of footsteps, while we were in all of the hangars stood completely still, was heard by everyone present.

The ghostly pilot of this air sea rescue helicopter is known to push people.
(By kind permission of the North East Aircraft Museum)

One of the team thought she heard someone singing '*Roll out the Barrels*', however she failed to mention this until later, as she thought it was someone in the Three Horseshoes pub next to the museum. She also saw a person looking at her from the cockpit of the helicopter in Hangar Two.

We set up a trigger object, some old coins. We drew around them on a piece of paper, and an hour later when we went back discovered that they had all moved. The North East Aircraft Museum, in our opinion, did not disappoint.

I also took the time to talk to Lee Foster of the Hauntedland Paranormal Research website (*www.hauntedland.co.uk*), and he explained to me what happened when he joined an investigation at the museum:

In March 2007, I attended a paranormal investigation at the North East Aircraft Museum. My experience was one of mixed feelings even though medium Ian Shillito headed it and tried his best to keep everyone entertained.

I went with an open mind in the hope that the reputation of it being one of the most active locations was true. Certainly, when the lights are off it does take on a whole new atmosphere as the silhouettes of huge planes and helicopters dominate the floor space.

There were a few things that occurred that failed to impress me, such as a model plane suspended on a wire which turned ever so slowly, seemingly at the mediums request – but it continued to do so anyway when he didn't! The EMF metre went off the scale at a particular location even though it is claimed, although not proven, that there is no electrical device or cabling in the area. Also the taps and cracks that occurred could have merely been stones and refuse thrown about by the unusually high winds that battered the hangers that night, not communication responses as some people claimed.

But there were some things that occurred that did impress me. The first was in the Westland helicopter. As we all sat in the darkness of the cabin, I suddenly felt travelsick as though we were flying along at great speed. Next door in a smaller hanger is a De Havilland Sea Venom. This is claimed to judder and move of its own accord, and sure enough, as I stood with my hands rested on its wing, it did vibrate slightly – but whether this is paranormal in a spiritual way remains questionable.

During a séance in the shop area, I did see on the opposite side of the room, a dim glow of white light that I put down to someone occasionally checking their watch with its light. When the lights came on however, no one was there; everyone was sitting on the floor!

My final experience was while I sat in the Gill Air Short 330. Ian, who was sat in front of me, said something had touched his head at the same moment I saw a tiny white light float above his head. As I reached out to hold it in my hand it disappeared.

Whether my experiences were genuine or psychological phenomena remains undecided though I do tend to side with the latter view. I'm sure those planes have a story to tell but on this night they weren't sharing it.

Visitor Information

Address:
North East Aircraft Museum
Old Washington Road
Sunderland
Tyne and Wear
SR5 3HZ

Tel: 0191 5190662
Email: info@neam.org.uk
Website: www.neam.org.uk

Opening Hours: 1 April–31 October, daily 10 a.m.–5 p.m.; 1 November–31 March, daily 10 a.m.–dusk
Closed Christmas Day, Boxing Day and New Year's Day
Last admission is one hour before closing

How to Get There: The museum is signposted from the A19

Additional Information:
• School and group visits can be arranged. Please contact the museum for details
• The NEAM shop stocks light snacks and refreshments

The Old Assembly Rooms

*B*uilding began on the Newcastle Assembly Rooms on 16 March 1764 at a cost of £6,700. Funding came from 129 shareholders holding 234 shares at the cost of £25 each and the Newcastle Corporation contributing a further £200. It was opened on 24 June 1776 as a meeting place for the city's high society.

The Assembly Rooms were designed by William Newton, the most successful architect in Newcastle in his day. They were built in a Georgian design and seven Rococo chandeliers were fitted. They were built locally in Newcastle and comprised of 10,000 pieces of hand-cut crystal.

Charles Dickens performed three playlets here on 27 August 1852, and Strauss gave a concert on 21 October 1838. The Assembly Rooms has received many royal visitors over the years including Edward VII, George V, and George VI

In 1967, the Old Assembly Rooms fell into disrepair and with no buyers wishing to take on the run-down and vandalised building. It looked likely that the building would be demolished in 1974. However, two brothers bought it and spent £250,000 restoring it to its former glory, and it has remained in the Michaelides family ever since.

Despite all the joyous occasions that the Old Assembly Rooms has seen, there was one night in particular where a dark, despicable act took place which cost an innocent young woman her life. On 31 December 1777, some wealthy young men were in one of the upstairs room seeing in the New Year. They were very drunk, and one of the young men demanded that his wife dance naked for his friends, she refused and he slapped her hard across the face. She did what was asked, but afterwards she was so humiliated that she walked slowly to the top of the spiral staircase and then threw herself off the musician's gallery to her death on the ballroom floor below.

The spirit of the woman remains in the Old Assembly Rooms to this day, noticeable by the rustling sound of a taffeta ball dress, and the scent of lavender. Staff have also experienced the sensation of being watched.

The Old Assembly Rooms.

Visitor Information

Address:
The Assembly Rooms
Fenkle Street
Newcastle-upon-Tyne
NE1 5XU

Tel: 0191 2328695
Website: www.assemblyrooms.co.uk
Email: functions@assemblyrooms.co.uk

How to Get There: The Old Assembly Rooms is in the centre of Newcastle and can be accessed from Clayton Street and Grey Street. It is also less than a five minute walk from Newcastle's Central railway station

Additional Information:
- The Assembly Rooms is the perfect venue for conferencing, banquets, and weddings; please contact the Assembly Rooms or see their website for further details
- Christmas Parties can be arranged at the Assembly Rooms for small parties of as few as ten people, or larger functions for up to 400 people

The Old George

Situated in the Cloth Market, in the heart of Newcastle's famous Bigg Market, the Old George is a popular public house dating back to the seventeenth century. It was once a coaching inn and retains the original wooden beams and low ceiling.

Charles I drank at the Old George in 1646 on a number of occasions. Charles was being held captive by the Scots on Pilgrim Street, but they allowed him to go and play a round of golf on the Shieldfield. He would stop off at the coaching inn for a drink. The chair that he sat in while drinking at the Old George remains to

The interior of the Old George. (By kind permission of the Old George)

this day in the 'Charles I Room'. Over the years many visitors have claimed to see the hazy outline of a ghostly figure sat in the chair.

In the bar footsteps have been heard by staff when the bar has been closed and no one else has been present, the footsteps seem to get closer and then just stop. A man with a dog has also been seen several times standing at the bar, upon being approached the man and his faithful hound vanish.

In the main function room staff have reported feeling nauseous, and have a constant feeling of being watched. Many members of staff are reluctant to go into the room alone.

Visitor Information

Address:
The Old George
Cloth Market
Newcastle-upon-Tyne
NE1 1EE

Tel: 0191 2693061

Opening Hours: Monday–Thursday midday–11 p.m., Friday and Saturday 11 a.m.–1.30 a.m., Sunday 7 p.m.–10.30 p.m.

How to Get There: The Old George is found in the Cloth Market, in the Bigg Market in the centre of Newcastle

Additional Information:
- Meals are available Monday–Thursday midday–4 p.m., Friday–Saturday midday–6 p.m.
- The function room is available to be booked for parties at no cost
- All major sporting events are shown live, including Sky football matches
- There is regular live music in the bar, with no cover charge
- Outside seating available in the summer

Souter Lighthouse

Souter lighthouse was the first lighthouse in the world powered by electrical alternators when it was opened in 1871. Standing over 75ft high, it was designed by James Douglass and built by Robert Allison of Whitburn. The decision was made to erect a lighthouse after twenty ships ran aground in the area in 1860. Some of these 'accidents' were down to locals who had taken to standing on the cliff tops shining lights out to sea to lure ships towards the rough ground, the cliffs, and Marsden Rock, a large piece of rock which had come away from the cliff face due to erosion. The locals would then loot the valuables on board once the crew

Souter Lighthouse at dusk. (By kind permission of the National Trust)

had abandoned the wrecked vessel. The name Souter came from the decision to construct the lighthouse at Souter Point, although the location was later changed and the lighthouse was actually built at Lizard Point a mile to the north. The light is made of four-and-a-half tons of glass, sat upon one-and-a-half tons of mercury. The light generated could be seen for up to twenty-six miles.

The lighthouse was decommissioned in 1988, and today it is run by the National Trust. The lighthouse keeper's living quarters, the engine room, and the light tower are all open to the public. The foghorn is still in working order, and is sounded throughout the year during special events.

The lighthouse is said be haunted by the spirit of a former lighthouse keeper, as well as the ghost of a man called Bob who was a colliery worker who lived, and died, in Souter Lighthouse in the 1930s. Both appear to be benign spirits and the staff, who have came to accept their presence, do not feel as if the ghosts of Souter Lighthouse are in any way threatening.

Staff have reported items vanishing throughout the lighthouse. They have looked high and low for the item, only for it to appear back where they thought that they had left it in the first place. The most common occurrence of these disappearing objects is in the engine room where tools often vanish; this has been reported to coincide with a strong smell of tobacco smoke.

A strange figure has been seen walking along the corridor which leads to the staircase of the light tower itself; this has been witnessed by both staff, and visitors.

In the kitchen female members of staff have been grabbed by unseen hands, and cutlery has been forcefully pulled from people's hands.

Visitor Information

Address:
Souter Lighthouse
Coast Road
Whitburn
Sunderland
Tyne and Wear
SR6 7NH

Tel: 01670 773966 (infomation line)
  0191 5293161

Opening Hours: March–November, 11 a.m.–5 p.m.
Open Good Friday
Last admission is at 4.30 p.m.

How to Get There: Two-and-a-half miles south of South Shields and five miles north of Sunderland on the A183 coast road

Additional Information:
- There is a National Trust Shop
- Dogs are allowed in the grounds, but must be kept on leads
- There is free parking less than 100yds away. The car park barrier is locked at set times in the evening – please see notices at entrance
- There is a tea room with home-made food
- Two holiday cottages on the south side of a complex of buildings attached to the shore-based working lighthouse. Sleeps four people. Available for short breaks and week bookings
- Immediately to the north is The Leas, two-and-a-half miles of beach, cliff and grassland with spectacular views, and flora and fauna. To the south is Whitburn Coastal Park, with coastal walks to the Whitburn Point Local Nature Reserve

The Sunderland Empire Theatre

The Empire Palace, as it was originally called, was opened on 1 July 1907 by Vesta Tilley, a popular music hall entertainer of the day, and one of the country's top male impersonators. She was also the first artist to perform at the theatre. The theatre's 90ft-high tower featured a revolving sphere topped by a statue of Terpsicore, the muse of music and dance.

The theatre closed in 1959 due to the growing popularity of television and cinema. Sunderland Council bought the theatre and reopened it the following year. Shortly after the reopening, the Beatles played at the Empire during their first UK tour.

On 26 April 1976, the famous *Carry On* actor Sid James suffered a massive heart attack early into the opening show of *The Mating Season*. An ambulance was called but Sid James didn't survive the journey to the hospital; he died shortly after leaving the building.

The ghost of Sid James is said to haunt dressing room number 1 that he occupied on the night of his death. A number of stars are believed to have experienced unusual happenings in the room ever since. In 1989, Les Dawson was appearing at the Sunderland Empire and was so disturbed by something that he witnessed in the dressing room that he asked to be moved rooms. He refused to talk about what had happened, and the press reported that he had seen the ghost of Sid James. Dawson refused to comment on what had actually happened on that night and took his secret to the grave.

Whereas Sid James is unquestionably the Empire's most famous ghost, the theatre is also reputedly haunted by the spirits of two females; Vesta Tilley, who opened the theatre over a century ago, and Molly Moselle. On 14 January 1949, Moselle, assistant stage manager to a touring company performing *The Dancing Years* at the Empire, left the building to go and post a birthday card and was never seen again. A few years ago a badly decomposed skeleton was fished out of the Wear, and it was obvious it had been in there for many years. It was the body of a female, roughly the same height as Molly, but the skeleton's identity could not be established.

Staff and visitors to the theatre regularly report feelings of being watched, and odd noises have been heard by staff in the auditorium when it's been empty. Footsteps have also been heard walking across the empty stage.

*The Sunderland Empire Theatre. (Photograph provided courtesy of
the Sunderland Empire Theatre)*

The auditorium. (Photograph provided courtesy of the Sunderland Empire Theatre)

Mr Melvyn James has worked at the Empire since 1972, and is the current technical manager. On that fateful night in 1976 which saw Sid James suffer a fatal heart attack, Melvyn was the first person to come to his aid. He was kind enough to take the time to tell me his memories of the passing of one of Britain's best-loved comics:

I was stage manager of the theatre, and it was the first day of the show. The cast, including Sid James, had been chatting and joking at the side of the stage before the performance began. I was in my office when, about ten minutes into the show the wardrobe mistress, Helen Lamb, came running to my door saying something had happened.

The stage was a box set in those days, meaning that the stage itself was separated from the wings. Sid was due on stage, but had not appeared. He was to walk up a few steps then down some more onto the set which was made up to look like a lounge. My office was close to the stage so I was there in seconds and I could see him slumped over at the side of the stage. I quickly climbed a ladder and then clambered onto a small perch and closed the curtains. The actress on stage, Olga, was shaking and said she wasn't sure if he was playing or if he was genuinely ill. I was the first person to him and straight away I knew from my basic first-aid knowledge from my time in the forces that there was nothing I could do for him. I went out onto the stage in front of a bemused audience and asked if there was a doctor in the house. The response was a huge laugh from a crowd who thought that this was part of the show. I persevered and fortunately there was a doctor in attendance and he came to the side of the stage. Everything happened so quickly, and by the time the doctor came to Sid's aid, the ambulance had also arrived. The ambulance crew didn't want to move him, but the doctor knew how serious it was and had him taken to the ambulance straight away.

Within the next hour or so we heard that tragic news that he had died. There was no understudy for him so the whole tour was cancelled; I mean how do you replace someone like Sid James? The set stayed on the stage for the remainder of the week until it was dismantled.

I've never seen or experienced anything that would lead me to believe that Sid James haunts the Empire, but I have read and heard reports that many believe that he does. The scariest thing I can recall was in 1972, the year I started working here. Back in those days the gallery, or 'the Gods' as some people call it, was closed off acoustically with a large curve going to the ceiling which would take the acoustics around the building, and the gallery was used for storage. I went up there one night with no lights on, just a torch, and for no apparent reason the hairs on the back of my neck stood up rigid like a stiff broom. I always felt uneasy in the gallery and would take someone with me if I needed to go up there.

Visitor Information

Address:
Sunderland Empire Theatre
High Street West
Sunderland
SR1 3EX

Tel: 0191 5661040
Website: www.sunderlandempire.org.uk
Email: sunderland.boxoffice@livenation.co.uk (Booking Enquiries)

Opening Hours: Opening times vary depending on performances. Please visit the theatre's website for event information

How to Get There: The theatre is in Sunderland city centre and is signposted on all routes into the city

Additional Information:
- The theatre can be booked for corporate hospitality and conferencing
- The Sunderland Empire has five bars. Interval drinks can be pre-ordered at any bar. Tea and coffee facilities are also available
- The theatre is equipped with a loop system
- There is an array or merchandise available to purchase for most performances including T-shirts, DVDs and CDs. Theatre memorabilia is also available to buy from the theatre kiosk

The Theatre Royal

The original Theatre Royal opened on 21 January 1788 on Mosley Street. However, within fifty years of the theatre's opening a decision was made for the theatre to be closed. It was on the route of Grey Street and obstructed Richard Grainger's bold redevelopment plans for the centre of Newcastle. The original theatre's final performance was on 25 June 1836.

The current Theatre Royal was built on Grey Street and was designed by local architects John and Benjamin Green. It opened it's doors on 20 February 1837 with a performance of William Shakespeare's *The Merchant of Venice*. The bells of St Nicholas' Church rang in celebration of the opening night.

In 1899 the theatre was ravaged by a huge fire after a performance of *Macbeth*. The interior of the building was completely destroyed. Theatre architect Frank Matcham redesigned the interior and it was reopened on 31 December 1901. The building is exactly the same externally as it was when it was first built.

Between 1986 and 1988 the theatre underwent a major refurbishment costing over £6.5million, reopening on 11 January 1988 with a performance of *A Man For All Seasons*, starring Charlton Heston.

The Theatre Royal dominates Newcastle's Grainger town to this day, and is a Grade I listed building. The Theatre Royal presents over 380 performances to over 300,000 people each year and is the regional home of the Royal Shakespeare Company.

In the nineteenth century the theatre offered cheap seats in the gallery to the lower classes. One lady who attended the theatre reguarly developed an infatuation with a handsome actor who was the leading man in a Victorian play at the theatre. She made an effort to see the play as often as she could afford. One night she decided to wait for him by the stage door and they began an affair. News of this scandal quickly spread and the pair decided to elope after his final performance and get married. The lady couldn't be happier, and she prepared to leave her life in Newcastle behind to be with the man she loved. The pair met after the penultimate performance of the play, the lady bursting with excitement and keen to discuss their future together. The man dropped a bombshell that was to break the lady's heart. He was already married and explained that his relationship with her was just a fling while he was in Newcastle. Heartbroken, she went to his final performance of the play.

The Theatre Royal. (By kind permission of the Theatre Royal)

The auditorium. (Photograph by Sally Ann Norman, provided courtesy of the Theatre Royal)

Tears were streaming down her face as the play neared it's climax, she couldn't take anymore. She threw herself from the gallery down into the packed stalls below, and to her death.

It is believed that it is this betrayed woman who still haunts the auditorium, she is known as the Grey Lady. She is often seen as a faint figure holding a lit candle. The sound of weeping, and deep sighing, has been heard throughout the theatre.

Visitor Information

Address:
Theatre Royal
100 Grey Street
Newcastle-upon-Tyne
NE1 6BR

Tel: 0844 8112121
Website: www.theatreroyal.co.uk
Email: boxoffice@theatreroyal.co.uk

How to Get There: The theatre is in the middle of Newcastle-upon-Tyne; a two minute walk from Grey's Monument

Additional Information:
- The theatre's website has up to date listings of all events, including shows, pantomimes, tours and talks
- There are regular sign-languaged, captioned, and audio described shows, for further information please visit the website
- One free ticket for the assistant of a disabled person who is not able to attend events unaccompanied
- There are eight wheelchair spaces available in the Stalls
- There is a sound enhancement system in the auditorium. Using a headset (with or without a hearing aid) you can boost the volume of the performance. Headsets are bookable at the Box Office, which has an induction loop
- Guide, hearing and other working dogs are welcome in all parts of the theatre
- Disabled toilets on every floor
- There is lift access to all levels of the theatre

The Town Moor

*T*he Town Moor is a large area of common land in Newcastle-upon-Tyne. It covers an area of almost 150 acres, stretching from the city centre and Spital Tongues in the south, up to Gosforth to the north, Kenton to the west, and Jesmond to the east. Every June locals flock to the Town Moor to visit 'The Hoppings', the largest travelling funfair in Europe. Despite the fun and laughter that is experienced annually when the fair is in town, the Town Moor has a dark history of death and anguish.

The Town Moor. (By kind permission of Newcastle City Council and the Freemen of Newcastle)

In the early fourteenth century the Town Moor was chosen as the location for Newcastle's gallows. Hangings drew huge crowds from miles around and were treated as great family entertainment. Drink would flow and the onlookers were baying for blood by the time the condemned criminal had the noose placed around their neck. The crowd would reach fever pitch as the felon dangled by the neck until dead.

Many hundreds of men and women were executed on the Moor for a variety of crimes, including horse and sheep stealing, highway robbery, burglary, rape, and murder. The last execution on the Town Moor took place on Friday 23 August 1844 when Mark Sherwood was hanged for the brutal murder of his wife, Ann.

One of the most bizarre executions occurred on 22 September 1752, when Ewan MacDonald, a Scottish soldier, was hanged on the Town Moor. MacDonald had been sentenced to death after killing a man, Robert Parker, in a heated argument at the Black Bull Inn in the Bigg Market. MacDonald was hanged before a crowd of thousands who saw him die. His body was cut down and taken to the Surgeon's Hall for dissection, a common practice. However, as an apprentice surgeon prepared to make the first incision into the corpse which lay on the table before

The Hoppings, the largest travelling fair in Europe. (By kind permission of Newcastle City Council and the Freemen of Newcastle)

him, MacDonald suddenly sat up and opened his eyes, miraculously rising from the dead. The terrified surgeon reached for a mallet and struck MacDonald's skull hard several times ensuring he would not get up again.

In 1649, the citizens of Newcastle, fearful of witchcraft, handed a petition to Newcastle Council requesting a witch-finder be brought in to rid the town of witches. In December of the same year a witch-finder arrived in Newcastle. His identity is not recorded, but it has been suggested that it may have been the infamous Scottish witch-finder John Kincaid. A bell ringer walked through the streets calling for anyone who was suspected of being a witch be brought to the town hall to be judged by the witch-finder. Thirty women were brought forward and the witch-finder tested them for involvements in witchcraft by 'pricking', the act of sticking a pin into various parts of the body, and if that person did not bleed from the wound then they guilty of being a witch.

Witch-finders were paid handsomely for their work and would become proficient in locating warts, or areas of hard skin on a person's body knowing that it was less likely to bleed. Twenty-seven women were found guilty and held at Newgate Gaol to await their fate. The records of the witch trials of 1649–1650 have not survived, but it is known that fifteen women and one man were hanged on the Town Moor on 21 August 1650 for witchcraft; their bodies were buried in unmarked graves in St Andrew's churchyard.

The Town Moor has a long history of ghost sightings, often coming from dog walkers and joggers who frequent the moorland. Witnesses describe seeing dark shadows moving swiftly before dispersing. Screams have also been heard, carried on the wind, across the Town Moor. Given how many people were executed here it seems the land may be stained forever by the loss of life that it has borne witness to for over 500 years.

Visitor Information

How to Get There: The Town Moor covers a wide area of the city. The Hoppings take place on the large area of land just outside of Newcastle city centre accessible from Great North Road (B1318)

Additional Information:
- During the annual visit of the Hoppings, there is car parking available on the Town Moor. Entrance to the car park is from Grandstand Road (A187)

Tynemouth Priory and Castle

On a headland at the mouth of the River Tyne stands Tynemouth Priory. Set against a beautiful seascape, this site has a long history of religion, beginning with an Anglian monastery which was built in AD 617. The early Northumbrian kings were buried at the monastery including St Oswin who died in AD 651. The monastery was set ablaze in the year AD 800 during a Viking raid. The site was strengthened due to the risk of future attacks. The next attack came in AD 832, but was averted. The Vikings raided the monastery successfully in AD 865, and a large number of nuns who had come to the Tynemouth, for the safety they believed it

Tynemouth Castle. (By kind permission of English Heritage)

The remains of Tynemouth Priory. (By kind permission of English Heritage)

would offer, were mercilessly slaughtered. Another attack came in AD 870, and in AD 875 the monastery was completely destroyed.

Tynemouth was abandoned as a religious site until 1090 when the Earl of Northumberland, Robert de Mowbray, made the decision to re-found Tynemouth Priory. Work began on a new church and castle atop the rocky outcrop. Improvements and enlargements were made a little over a century later, including the 73ft-high presbytery which was added in 1190s.

In 1296, the need for defense increased and a stone wall was built to surround the site. A fortified gatehouse was later added to offer the priory further protection. In the fifteenth century the magnificent Percy Chantry was built, a small vaulted chapel.

In 1538 the monastery was disbanded and the monastic buidings, which now served no purpose, were destroyed. The church continued to be used until 1668 when a new church was built in nearby North Shields for the locals.

The castle and church at Tynemouth Priory began to decay, and the site was used for a number of different purposes over the years that followed. The church had became completely ruined by the turn of the eighteenth century, and was used as a burial ground with over 700 bodies being laid to rest there between 1715 and 1856.

The Percy Chantry. (By kind permission of English Heritage)

The interior of Tynemouth Castle. (By kind permission of English Heritage)

Tynemouth Priory and Castle on a snowy winter morning.

A lighthouse was built on the headland in 1775 using stone taken from the priory. This was demolished in 1895 when St Mary's Lighthouse was build along the coast at Whitley Bay. The castle functioned as a barracks in the late eighteenth and early nineteenth century, with coastal gun batteries being built. They were operational throughout both world wars.

During the twentieth century the north and east curtain walls collapsed and fell into the sea. The site is now managed by English Heritage.

With almost 1,400 years of history, including the horrific loss of life suffered in the ninth century, it is unsuprising that Tynemouth Priory and Castle is widely believed to be one of the most paranormally active locations in the north east.

The most well-known ghost is that of Olaf the Viking. During one of the early invasions in the ninth century, one Viking warrior was wounded and left for dead by his countrymen. The forgiving monks of Tynemouth took him in and nursed him back to health. The Viking was so indebted to the monks, that he embraced their faith and joined their order.

The Vikings invaded again several years later and the monks stood their ground, fighting against all odds, to defend their land. Olaf had left his murderous past behind and his loyalties lay firmly with his fellow monks. He fought like a true warrior, killing a number of the mauraders. Olaf saw a nearby Viking about to run his sword through an unarmed monk and acted quickly, killing the Viking in an instant. As the dead invader fell to the ground Olaf saw his face and to his horror realised he had killed his own brother.

Olaf fell to his knees, as the battle continued around him, and prayed to God to accept his brother's soul into heaven. Olaf was so overcome with grief that he too died, slumping to the ground alongside his dead brother's bloodied body.

It is believed that Olaf's ghost remains at Tynemouth Priory, and has been seen, both by day and night, looking out to sea.

There is a ninth-century stone known as the Monk's Stone near to the burial ground. It is weathered and worn, but designs of animals and scrolls can still be seen carved into it. A large number of people have reported seeing a monk knelt at this stone in prayer. He is described as wearing a brown robe with a gold belt.

Ghostly nuns have been seen walking across the site, often walking straight through walls of buildings. If these are ghosts of the murdered nuns of AD 865 then these structures would not have existed in their time, being built many centuries after their deaths.

Visitors to Tynemouth in search of the paranormal may find spending some time in Cullercoats beneficial. Cullercoats lies a mile along the coast and has a semi-circular bay with cliffs and a number of caves. Since the mid 1990s this sheltered bay has been the scene of a number of unusual sightings. People have claimed to see what can only be descibed as a prehistoric man wearing animal skin, with long matted hair, and bare feet. Little is known as to why the 'Cullercoats Caveman', as he has been nicknamed, appears on this stretch of coastline, or if he a living, breathing, flesh-and-blood 'man', or a ghost from a time long past.

Visitor Information

Address:
Tynemouth Priory and Castle
Tynemouth
Tyne and Wear
NE30 4BZ

Website: www.english-heritage.org.uk

Opening Hours: April–September, daily 10 a.m.–5 p.m.; October–March, Thursday–Monday 10 a.m.–4 p.m.
Closed 24–26 December and 1 January.
Opening dates change annually so please consult the website for further information

How to Get There: Tynemouth Priory and Castle is based in Tynemouth town centre next to the North Pier

Additional Information:
- There is no parking on site, but car parks are close by in the town centre and the North Pier
- Dogs are allowed on leads
- There is a gift shop. However, there are no refreshments available but picnics are welcome, and there are a variety of shops and takeaways in the town centre less than five minutes away on foot
- Suitable for wheelchairs users
- Tynemouth Priory and Castle are available to book for private and corporate events

Washington Old Hall

The first building on the site that Washington Old Hall now stands upon was a wooden Saxon hall dating back to the tenth century. In 1183, William de Hertburne assumed the lands at Wessington, and he became William de Wessynton, choosing the Norman-French spelling for his name, despite the estate being of Anglo-Saxon origin. He built the first stone manor house on the site of the previous hall. The village of Wessington later became known as Washington, and George Washington, the first President of the United States of America, was a direct descendent of the family.

The manor house stayed in the Washington family until the early fifteenth century, when Eleanor Washington died, leaving it to her daughter Dionisia, who

Washington Old Hall. (By kind permission of the National Trust)

then married a man by the name of Sir William Mallory. The Mallory family sold the house to William James, the Bishop of Durham, for £4,000 in 1613.

The Bishop died four years after purchasing the house, and it passed into the hands of the his son, Francis, who, in the period between 1613 and 1623, drastically rebuilt the house, demolishing much of the earlier building. The improved structure consisted of five bedrooms and a linen closet, and at the western end of the building stood a milk house and buttery. Although most of the original room divisions have long since been removed, the revamped manor house that Francis James built is how the house remains to this day in its present form.

During the late seventeenth century the building was let out to tenants, and by the late nineteenth century there were over thirty people living within the hall, which had fallen into a state of disrepair. By 1932 the Old Hall lay empty as it was in no state for human habitation, and in 1936 an order was issued for the building to be demolished. The locals formed a committee to increase awareness of Old Hall's importance, and raise funds in order to buy the ruined building. The committee included the local schoolmaster, Frederick Hill, and rector, Cyril Lomax.

The Preservation Committee successfully saved Washington Old Hall from being destroyed, but due to the war, work did not begin on the building until 1951. It was restored in the style of the Jacobean period and opened to the public in 1955.

The Great Hall. (By kind permission of the National Trust)

In 1956 the ownership of the building was entrusted to the National Trust to continue the work that the Preservation Committee had begun.

Washington Old Hall is said to be haunted by a ghostly female form. She is described as wearing a long grey dress and is said to 'glide' along the upper floor, often accompanied by the smell of lavender. No one is certain who this lady is and why she continues to haunt the Old Hall. It is also unknown if she is the same lady as the ghostly woman that has been seen weeping throughout the hall. Strange sounds have also been heard coming from the hall late at night.

Visitor Information

Address:
Washington Old Hall
The Avenue
Washington Village
Washington
Tyne and Wear
NE38 7LE

Tel: 0191 4166879
Website: www.nationaltrust.org.uk/main/w-washingtonoldhall
Email: washingtonoldhall@nationaltrust.org.uk

Opening Hours: March–November, 11 a.m.–5 p.m., Sunday–Wednesday
Last admission is 30 minutes before closing
Opening dates change annually so please consult the website for further information

How to Get There: From A19 or A1 join the A1231 and follow the brown signs for Washington Old Hall

Additional Information:
- There is a souvenir shop in the entrance
- Dogs are allowed in the garden on leads
- The tea room on the first floor sells light refreshments
- Washington Old Hall is licensed for weddings and is also suitable for wedding receptions. Please call for more information, or visit the website

The Wheatsheaf

Staff and customers at the Wheatsheaf public house in West Boldon have long suspected that the building, which dates back to the early nineteenth century, is home to a number of ghosts. There have been a lot of bizarre happenings reported, such as chairs being moved around, utensils in the kitchen being thrown across the room, people being pushed and touched, and screaming heard during the night. One shaken female customer was in the toilets when she looked in a mirror and saw the reflection of a young girl standing behind her, she turned around to see if the girl needed any help as she had blood on her face and looked to be in some distress, but upon turning around there was no one there.

The heavy industrial fridge doors are often found open, even though the kitchen door had been locked, and no one had accessed the room. Several years ago a hand print of a small child was found in a jelly, even though the kitchen had been locked, and no children were in the building.

Answers for these strange occurrences came in 2004 at a charity psychic evening, and the events that were to follow were so terrifying that they would not have been out of place in a Hollywood horror movie.

Professional medium Suzanne Hadwin had not been told of the paranormal occurrences, but picked up on an evil, angry, presence straight away and her mind was filled with visions of truly horrific crimes against children. Suzanne said that there were thirty-seven spirits within the premises, and one in particular was crying out for help.

Jessica Ann Hargreaves, a name previously unrelated to the Wheatsheaf, was six years old when her life was taken from her. Suzanne explained that Jessica had been taken to the cellar, raped, and then strangled to death by a man in his thirties called Joseph Lawrence, who she believed was the landlord, or a barman. After killing little Jessica, Joseph hacked her lifeless body to pieces and hid her body in the cellar in a large fireplace, later returning and moving her remains.

The malevolent spirit of Joseph Lawrence remains at the Wheatsheaf, eternally tormenting the ghost of young Jessica. Jessica wasn't the only victim of Joseph. Suzanne explained that he brutally killed eight other children within these walls. Suzanne described him as a vile, evil man, and the atmosphere within the building made her feel physically sick. It is also believed that he didn't always commit these despicable acts alone, sometimes working with two unnamed accomplices.

Jessica was a girl local to Sunderland, her mother was Kathleen, and her father was called Billy. Billy suspected Joseph of being involved in his daughter's disappearance and killed him.

Suzanne returned a few nights later in an attempt to release the tortured souls which reside here and to help them find peace and move on. Suzanne ran a tape recorder while trying to make contact with the spirits at the Wheatsheaf. She listened back to the tape and, in the presence of the staff, heard a male voice clearly say 'I'm coming for you Suzanne. I'm going to kill you Suzanne'.

Despite the threats against her life, Suzanne was determined to continue her work. Researching the pub's history at Boldon Library, Suzanne and a barman from the Wheatsheaf found records, including pictures, of both Jessica and Joseph.

Suzanne was confident she knew where Jessica's body had initially been hidden, and staff worked through the night knocking down a hollow interior wall, to reveal a previous unknown fireplace, exactly as Suzanne had been shown by Jessica. Within the fireplace they found a child's shoe, a torn piece of a dress, and a lock of hair.

The search for the eventual hiding place of Jessica's body continues.

The amazing events at the Wheatsheaf in 2004 led to it being voted the most haunted public house in the UK.

The Wheatsheaf Hotel.

Visitor Information

Address:
The Wheatsheaf
St Nicholas Road
West Boldon
Tyne and Wear
NE36 0QR

Tel: 0191 5363208

Opening Hours: Monday–Thursday 3 p.m.–11.30 p.m., Friday and Saturday 11.30 a.m.–midday, Sunday 11.30 a.m.–11.30 p.m.

How to Get There: The Wheatsheaf is on the A184 in West Boldon

Additional Information:
- A function room can be hired for free, complete with a free DJ. Please contact the Wheatsheaf for further details
- Home cooked food is available throughout the week midday–6 p.m., and a carvery is served on Sundays from midday

About the Author

Rob Kirkup was born in Ashington, Northumberland in 1979. He developed a keen interest in the paranormal from an early age, amassing a large collection of books and newspaper cuttings on the subject, and in particular stories of supernatural happenings in the North East of England.

In 2002 Rob led a paranormal investigation at Talkin Tarn, a haunted lake in Cumbria, as part of Alan Robson's Night Owls' Hallowe'en show on Metro Radio. In the years that have followed, Rob has conducted investigations at some of the North East's most haunted locations, including Hylton Castle, Woodhorn Church, Flodden Field, Chillingham Castle, and the Castle Keep.

Rob's first book, *Ghostly Northumberland*, was published in 2008 by The History Press. The third book in this series, *Ghostly County Durham*, will follow in 2010.

The author, Rob Kirkup.

Sources &c. Recommended Reading

Anderson, Maureen, *Executions and Hangings in Newcastle & Morpeth*, (Wharncliffe Books 2005)

Anderson, Maureen, *Foul Deeds & Suspicious Deaths in and around Newcastle*, (Wharncliffe Books 2004)

Bath, Jo, *Dancing with the Devil and Other True Tales of Northern Witchcraft*, (Tyne Bridge Publishing 2002)

Hallam, Jack, *Ghosts of the North*, (David & Charles 1976)

Hallowell, Michael J., *Ales and Spirits: The Haunted Pubs and Inns of South Tyneside*, (Sunderland: The People 2000)

Hallowell, Michael J., *The Mystery Animals of the British Isles: Northumberland and Tyneside*, (CFZ Press 2008)

Histon, Vanessa, *Ghosts of Grainger Town*, (Tyne Bridge Publishing 2001)

Jones, Richard, *Haunted Britain and Ireland*, (New Holland Publishers 2003)

Jones, Richard, *Haunted Castles of Britain and Ireland*, (New Holland Publishers 2005)

Jones, Richard, *Haunted Inns of Britain and Ireland*, Richard Jones (New Holland Publishers 2004)

Jones, Richard, *Haunted Houses of Britain and Ireland*, (New Holland Publishers 2005)

Liddell, Tony, *Otherworld North East – Ghosts and Hauntings Explored*, (Tyne Bridge Publishing 2004)

Linahan, Liz, *The North of England Ghost Trail*, (Constable 1997)

Ritson, Darren W., *Ghost Hunter: True-life Encounters from the North East*, (Grosvenor House Publishing Limited 2006)

Robson, Alan, *Grisly Trails and Ghostly Tales*, (Virgin Books 1992)

Robson, Alan, *Nightmare on Your Street*, (Virgin Books 1993)

Tegner, Henry, *Ghosts of the North Country*, (Butler Publishing 1991)

Warren, Melanie, and Wells, Tony, *Ghosts of the North*, (Broadcast Book 1995)

Other local titles published by The History Press

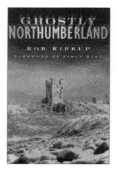

Ghostly Northumberland
ROB KIRKUP

Drawing on historical and contemporary sources, this collection of stories contains both well-known and hitherto unpublished tales from over twenty of the most haunted locations in Northumberland today, including a piano-playing ghost at Bamburgh Castle, the White Lady of Cresswell Tower, a mischievous poltergeist at the Schooner Hotel, as well as sightings of torturer John Sage, who continues to stalk the dungeons at Chillingham Castle – widely regarded to be one of the most haunted places in Britain.

978 0 7509 5043 5

Haunted Newcastle
DARREN W. RITSON

This collection of spooky tales takes the reader on a tour through the streets, cemeteries, alehouses and attics of Newcastle. It unearths a chilling range of supernatural phenomena, including the vampire rabbit of Collingwood House, the Pink Lady of Jesmond and the tale of the mysterious witches' bones. Illustrated with over sixty photographs, this book will delight everyone with an interest in the supernatural history of the area.

978 0 7524 4880 0

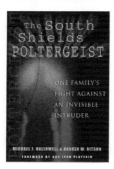

The South Shields Poltergeist
MICHAEL J. HALLOWELL & DARREN W. RITSON

Meticulously documented, *The South Shields Poltergeist* is a truly terrifying account which details the authors' struggle with an invisible, malicious entity that threatened and intimidated everyone who dared to stand up to it. Their encounter may well go down in the annals of psychical research as one of the most chilling true-life encounters of its kind.

978 0 7509 4874 6

Haunted Sunderland
RUPERT MATTHEWS

Ghost-hunter Rupert Matthews explores Sunderland's darkest secrets in this creepy collection of true-life tales. From the Ryhope Poltergeist and the White Lady of Washington Hall, to the glowing grave at Wingate and a spectral talking cat, he unearths a chilling range of supernatural phenomena. Illustrated with over eighty photographs, this book will delight everyone interested in Sunderland's haunted heritage.

978 0 7524 4663 9

If you are interested in purchasing other books published by The History Press, or in case you have difficulty finding any History Press books in your local bookshop, you can also place orders directly through our website
www.thehistorypress.co.uk